Tyrone E. Boyce is a writer, motivational speaker, and an economist with many years of experience in research and data analysis. He has a BSc in economics, a diploma in counselling, and a licentiate in theology. He writes all his speeches, some of which have earned him first place in several Toastmasters' competitions. Tyrone also writes copy as a freelancer and spends way too much time in front of his laptop; having his favorite Bar-B-Q ribs on weekends while writing. He is the author of the book *The Diamond Mentality – Living the Worry-Free Life*; the first in the series.

This book is dedicated to my four wonderful children: Rukiya, Rashidi, Runako and Ronnell.

I wrote this book so that you can have an understanding of the human potential to live life to the fullest. Society socialized us in a way that we embrace fear and this limits our power, and the potential to be the best that we can ever be. I charge you then to put God first in your life and remove all fear from you, for fear cripples. Stay far from gossip and gossipers and always have a positive attitude. Accept the things that you cannot change, stay away from evil and do that which is good. Love you dearly.

Tyrone E. Boyce

The Diamond Mentality

Living the Worry-Free Life

AUSTIN MACAULEY PUBLISHERS™

LONDON • CAMBRIDGE • NEW YORK • SHARJAH

Ordering Information
Quantity sales: Special discounts are available on quantity purchases by corporations, associations, and others. For details, contact the publisher at the address below.

Publisher's Cataloging-in-Publication data
Boyce, Tyrone E.
The Diamond Mentality

ISBN 9781643781242 (Paperback)
ISBN 9781641826976 (Hardback)
ISBN 9781641827690 (ePub e-book)

Library of Congress Control Number: 2021914576

www.austinmacauley.com/us

First Published (2021)
Austin Macauley Publishers LLC
40 Wall Street, 33rd Floor, Suite 3302
New York, NY 10005
USA

mail-usa@austinmacauley.com
+1 (646) 5125767

I am forever grateful to my God who planted this idea in me many years ago and who provided everything to show me how phenomenal it is. He also provided the right type of motivation at the perfect times when I felt like giving up. To Him, I give thanks first and foremost for without Him this book would not be possible. All the glory to God.

An extra special "thank you" to Esther, who tirelessly hung in there with me and although she underwent surgery while proofing the manuscript, she stuck with me to the end and never gave up. Even when I told her she didn't need to continue due to her pain and discomfort she insisted she will see it through to the end. Esther, you are a true friend. Love always.

Thanks goes out to Muriel who proofread four chapters. Your contribution was invaluable and I truly appreciate it.

To those who agreed to be interviewed and those who tested the concept and provided feedback, your contributions were invaluable and I thank you from the bottom of my heart. Without you, this work would not be complete.

The world is filled with wonderful people and Alex Wright from Reedsy is one of them. Though we never met in person, I want to give you a big thank you for all the tips and information you sent me regarding publishing. You never made me feel like I was a botherer. I truly thank you.

My friends from Naturopathic Toastmasters Club Drena, Wendy, Janice, Chayan and all the others who always checked in to see how I was progressing thereby indirectly making sure that I didn't give up. A special thanks to all of you.

To my publishers who worked tirelessly and patiently to produce the final product and to the marketing team whose expertise is second to none and did everything to make this magnificent book a success, a very special thanks to you.
Finally, I want to thank all you readers who will make this book a resounding success. For without you, for whom this book was written, it would not be a success.

Table of Contents

Introduction

While reading the Bible, I came across a verse that stated that we cannot add a single hour to our life by worrying. I then remembered the various scenes I saw in the places that I worked. People would agonize about work conditions, salary, unrealistic deadlines, co-workers' attitudes and many other issues. The common denominator was that worry did not change any of these things. After spending hours upset about the problem, the problem remained unsolved. This does not only apply to the workplace but to all areas of our life including our family, church, and the various social organizations that we are affiliated with. Worrying cannot add time to your life and it does not solve problems. It can, however, give you problems, health problems.

As a trained economist, I decided to research and investigate worry and stress and their impact on people and society. The results changed my life completely. There are many treatments for worry and stress including medication when it is severe. However, these treatments only control the symptoms but not the underlying root cause. Hence, when your doctor tells you to go on a relaxing vacation to help reduce your stress and make you feel better, he tells the truth. However, the stress problem returns soon after you return to work. Why? Because the solution the doctor gave only treated the symptoms not the cause of the stress.

We have been socialized to think and believe that worrying is just a normal and natural part of life and there is nothing we can do about it. We grew up seeing our parents and just about everyone else in our society worrying; so, we accept that it is a normal part of life.

Can we honestly say that something that makes us sick and even kills us is a normal part of life? Is it really okay to worry? We accept that it is okay to worry while at the same time, we are very concerned about stress. Worrying is the leading cause of stress. This major health risk can manifest itself in so many ways and contribute significantly to our ill-health and, in many cases, death.

Given that most people do not like to be sick and that stress is a significant contributor to illness, death and low productivity; It is clear that worrying is *not* a good thing and should not be accepted as a normal part of our lives. Eliminate worry and you eliminate negative stress and a whole lot of other problems from your lives.

We are the product of our experiences. They help to shape us into who we are. In most cases, we become hardened (set in our ways) by these experiences. Hard is good, diamonds are hard, but sometimes we become hardened, cold and mean. Do we want to become like that? No, don't ever allow anyone to cause you to become cruel and mean. You were wonderfully and beautifully made. Yes, you want to be tough and hard as a diamond, but you also want the diamond's beauty. Therefore, direct the knowledge and wisdom gained from your experiences to become a diamond: hard, shiny and beautiful.

The information that follows will show you how to deal with the root cause of your worry and stress. Once implemented in your life, it will significantly eliminate or reduce your stress. As a result, you will look younger, stress-related illnesses will be things of the past, and joy and happiness will return to your life. You will be more productive in all areas of your life, including the workplace.

Foreword

This book is like no other book on stress. While other books may tell or teach you how to relieve stress. This book does not do that. This book is about stress prevention by adopting specific attitudes and behaviors that will enable you to turn a toxic environment to your advantage. In other words, you will be able to transform the toxic waste of everyday living into fruitful and helpful matter. While others may encourage you to relieve your stress by getting a massage, taking a vacation, exercising, having sex regularly, getting adequate sleep, etc., this book goes deeper. It deals with the source of your stress so that you remain in control just as God created you to be in control, *Genesis 1:26*. If you desire a quick fix, then there are plenty of books out there that will tell you how to get a quick fix. Conversely, if you want back your life from sickness due to stress; if you want back your marriage and good relationship with others; if you want a quality life as your creator intended it, then read on. Do not only read about these six core behaviors but implement them into every area of your everyday life. Watch and feel the results as you live the life of a *diamond mentality*.

Chapter 1
What Is the Diamond Mentality?

"You sit around all day watching television. You do not look for work to support your family. You are not a good example to your children. They see you drunk, and you offer no type of guidance to them. You are just a loser; you have a very poor mentality," Kim shouted to her deadbeat husband.

So, what is a mentality? According to *Collins* dictionary, Your mentality is your *attitudes or ways of thinking. Dictionary.com* defines mentality as *the characteristic attitude of mind or way of thinking of a person or group.* There is consistency among the various dictionaries as to what a mentality is.

It is well-known that our ways of thinking affect our actions and our actions influence our outcomes. That is why some people appear to us as expected, some as strange or abnormal, and others as extraordinary. All because of their mentalities. We all have a mentality, yet our mentalities are different. Our mentality is influenced by our families, social institutions like schools, religious institutions, and our experiences.

Despite the necessary external influences on our mentalities, we control how our mentalities are crafted. We are not slaves to our psyche. We get to decide who and how we are. Unfortunately, some of us are socialized to believe that we are what we are, which cannot be changed. However, there are many documentations in this world to show that is not true. People who were criminals and drug addicts have changed their mindset to become successful. Others who didn't think much of themselves took a round-about turn, changed their mentality, and achieved their dreams.

Your mentality will determine your level of success. What makes mentality so interesting is that although your mentality determines your level of success, you get to decide the type of mentality you have. Hence, you have control over your success or lack thereof. The lack of this vital piece of knowledge, that you control your mentality results in many people believing they cannot change. *Hosea 4:6 (NRSV)* states: "My people are destroyed for lack of knowledge." Due to the lack of this vital piece of information, many people destroy their lives or never reach their full potential. You have full control over your mentality and who you will become.

Take, for example, Roland and Shirland. Roland was doing very well for himself. He had a university degree and held the position of marketing manager. The firm had to downsize, and Roland's post was made redundant. With no job and a family to take care of, Roland just thought it was the end of the world. He couldn't handle the pressure, and he lost his mind and ended up in a mental institution. Luckily for him, his wife took charge and was able to take care of the collapsing family. However, Roland was never the same again and was always in and out of a mental institution.

Shirland was also well educated and had his bachelor's as well. He was an executive manager at an insurance company. Another insurance company bought the company for which he worked. As a result, some positions, mostly duplicate positions, were eliminated, and Shirland was made redundant after fifteen years at that company. Shirland had three children to take care of and a wife who was in a low-income job.

Shirland did not give up in the face of defeat but fought back with all he had. He went to a bank and successfully acquired a loan to open his own company; an investment company. That company quickly grew and was doing profitable business with most of the major banks and insurance companies. Shirland was able to continue to take care of his family and was in a much better position than before. He took the negative that stared him in the face and threatened to defeat him. He turned it into positive, into victory for him and his family.

Severe problems that could happen to any of us at any time confronted both Roland and Shirland. However, their mentalities were different, and as a result, their outcomes were different. It is interesting to note that Roland also had a diploma in electronics technology and was very good at repairing televisions and radios, which he did as a hobby. However, when calamity came calling, it was as though he forgot about his other talents that he could have used. If we allow them, fear and stress can shut down our minds and prevent us from thinking clearly.

Pauline is a friend of mine who loves to admire successful people. Pauline will say to me, "Tyrone, I admire you so much. You never give up. With the odds against you, you were able to go to university. You work in a profession that pays well and you also have your own business." She would then continue the conversation by talking about another person that she admires.

I would say to Pauline, "You too can achieve great things. You just need to dream and have a passion to see your dream come to reality. That passion would propel you to achieve whatever you desire."

Pauline would respond, "Me? Oh no. I am not as smart as you all. I don't have the brains; I will never amount to anything much."

Pauline saw herself like that because of her mentality and her attitude towards herself. She just didn't see herself in a positive light. However, from talking to Pauline over the years, I knew she was smart. I will dare say she was even more intelligent than me. She just didn't have confidence in herself; she didn't believe in herself the way she did in others.

Some people believe they will never amount to anything and never try. Others would try but give up at the first sign of difficulty or obstacles. On the other hand, some set the sky as their limit and will plow forward even in the face of defeat because surrender is not an option.

Take Linda, for instance. Linda was diagnosed with lupus from age 7, and the doctors had told her mum that she wouldn't make it to age 16. Linda proved them all wrong. Despite her sickness, Linda had a dream to be a nurse, and she didn't let the threat of death over her head stop her from going after her dream. Linda successfully completed her nursing program and became a registered nurse. Then she wanted a child, so she fell in love and got pregnant, against the doctor's advice that it would put her life and the child's life in danger. Linda ignored everyone and bore a healthy baby boy who is now a young, healthy man of 26 years. To date (2018), Linda is now 48, still living with lupus, and loves a good laugh. It was her mentality that did not allow her circumstances to dictate her reality. She understood that God was the author of her life.

Many people would have surrendered to their sickness and probably said something like, "It makes no sense, I could die any day." I have news for you all. There are many considered to be healthy who drop dead daily, just like the unhealthy. Tomorrow is promised to no one, sick or healthy. Linda has lived longer than many "healthy" people.

You live your life interacting with all types of people, and sometimes you ask yourself why this person behaves the way they do? Why are some people so mean? Why are some people so kind and generous? The answer lies in their mentality. Some people allow their circumstances to decide who they will become. In contrast, others determine that outside influences will not control them.

There are many factors that influence our behavior. The most important of these are our attitudes and or mentality. Of course, your attitudes are influenced by your parents, teachers, religion, friends, and the various organizations with which we are affiliated. Your mentality, which is the sum of all your outlooks to the various things in life, is influenced and shaped by your attitudes. Very important to note, people and circumstances can significantly impact your attitudes. Still, ultimately you have the final say in what and who shapes your attitudes. That is why some of us are loving and kind, while others are full of hatred and anger.

You are the product of your experiences. Intentional or unintentional, some people allow their experiences to determine who they will become. Some people become hardened, angry, and cold as a result of their experiences. Others become more loving, kind, and forgiving.

Two persons may face similar problems or challenges. In the end, one emerges more optimistic, having a better understanding of life and appreciating life and people more, being kind, generous and loving. While the other become submerged in negativity, embracing hatred and unleashing unkindness. In the first case, that person looked to see what they could learn from the situation and how they could turn the negative around for their good and the good of others. The other person allowed the problem to act on them, get the better of them and focused only on the negative situation. Rather than choose for themselves, they let the predicament choose for them. Negative situations will always choose negatively for you. If you want a different result, then you have to decide for yourself. Never allow your circumstances to dictate your future reality. When you don't choose, you are permitting your circumstances to choose for you.

Trevor and the hiring manager were very close friends. A lady came to the office on a temporary assignment to fill a vacant position for a person on leave. As the work came near its end, the young lady asked Trevor to talk to the hiring manager on her behalf as she had applied for a vacant position at the office. Trevor, who had become friends with the lady, spoke to the manager on her behalf. The manager did hire her, although she had a few reservations about the young lady. In less than six months, the lady became aggressive towards Trevor and started to come against him. The situation escalated and left Trevor a changed person. Trevor became bitter and vowed that he would never again help anyone to get a job.

David told me his story of how a woman came to his department and asked for his help in getting a permanent position. He helped her, and she was hired. Later, she also turned on him. David was hurt by the situation and was initially furious. However, he decided it was in his best interest to forgive the lady, which he did. As a result, David chose to continue helping others wherever possible. He would not allow anyone to cause him to become bitter and unkind.

The type of mentality you have is critical to you and everyone you interact with. I am sure you would have heard someone referred to another person's mentality as either positive or negative. People will want to draw close to you or distance themselves from you because of their perception of your mentality.

As *Collins* dictionary points out, your mentality is your attitudes. Put differently, your mentality is the sum of your attitudes. Yes, you do have many different attitudes. That is why a person may say I like your attitude towards work. Then because you speak in the negative, they may say you have a very negative attitude. So, you see, you can have a good attitude towards work but a negative attitude as it relates to outcomes.

There is good news! You determine your attitude and hence your mentality. Your experiences influence them, but you have the final say. Just because you have had a bad experience is no reason to have a bad attitude towards that thing, or anything. You can choose to be positive regardless. Society may want to tell us differently, but you get to decide. It is you that make that final choice as to your attitude. Not making a choice is actually making a choice. Whether you deliberately make a choice or leave it to chance, your attitude will be determined. You will most likely end up with a bad attitude towards whatever it is or towards everything. That is why it is imperative to make choices deliberately. It means that you determine your outcomes and not some bad experience or some other person.

Life is full of stressful situations. These stressful situations can arise in your household, at work, commuting, at the club, and many other places. Stressful situations are unavoidable and leave you feeling drained of energy at the end of the day. Some people are driven to suicide due to stressful situations they thought they could no longer cope with.

Stress can also wreak havoc on your health and can trigger a variety of illnesses. Sometimes, the physician cannot trace the root cause of the sickness back to stress. As a result, the medication prescribed does not work, resulting in a prolonged illness. If this sounds like you or you know of someone that fits into these categories, let them know that they don't have to live a life full of stress.

Society taught us that there isn't anything we can do about it. Take a vacation, they say, and that will help. And it does…but then after the holiday, you go right back to the stressful situation, and within a few days, or weeks, you feel totally stressed-out again. The Creator gave you control over your life. You can start by rejecting the lies you have been told repeatedly, that you have no control. You go to the doctor and he medicates you. That temporarily helps to control your stress but with numerous side effects. You are an intelligent being capable of making wise choices to choose to eliminate or minimize the stress in your life.

To eliminate stress from your life, you need *The Diamond Mentality*. To have a happy life, you need *The Diamond Mentality*. To have a peaceful life, you need *The Diamond Mentality*.

So, what is the diamond mentality? The diamond mentality is a way of thinking that pivots you from the standard mode of thinking. You become equipped with the ability to withstand life's problems and challenges and live a worry-free life. The diamond mentality is a solutions-driven mindset, a motivational and inspirational life.

The diamond mentality is living a life free of mental bondages. It is not living a "don't care-ish life." That is, you become hardened and don't care about anyone or anything. On the contrary, you are God's Creation, and so your heart is filled with the love of God for all humanity regardless of class, creed, or color. You care about people and what happens to them.

The diamond mentality equips you with the tools to respond to the problems and challenges in your life each day in such a way that results in you becoming worry-free. You may ask, but how is that possible? I say, continue to read, and you will find out how to change your mentality to a "diamond mentality" that will empower you to live your life free from worry.

The essence of the diamond mentality is to empower you to live your life free from worry and hence make you more productive in the workplace. It gives you and your family a much happier lifestyle. As a result of the stress-free life, you look younger, so there is no need for any expensive plastic surgery. You can live a life where every part of your life is simply incredible! Your smile is natural and genuine. Happiness flows from your heart like a river flowing down a mountain, and every person you come into contact with is positively affected by your effervescent mentality.

For example, a person without the diamond mentality, who had a painful experience like breaking-up with a partner, may respond so that it leaves no room for reconciliation in the near or distant future. Unnecessary harsh words are spoken, and wounds are opened, leaving life-long scars. "Why did this happen to me?" you may ask. "Bad things are always happening to me. It is as if I am a magnet for bad things; why was it so severe, couldn't it have happened another way or another day?"

These are just some of the things that we keep playing over and over in our minds. As a result, we create more stress the longer we take to find a solution, and the longer we worry, the more our health will be affected.

A person with the diamond mentality would handle the situation with love and tenderness. Words of peace, love, and forgiveness replace harsh and insulting remarks. This positive response reduces the amount of hurt and stress. It paves the way for quick healing and possible reconciliation in the future.

With the diamond mentality, you will accept what has happened and take responsibility for your actions. Recognize that the other person has a choice and that you should respect their choice if you genuinely love them, even if that means that you are excluded from their life. Forgive the person and focus on the good times of the relationship. Wish the person the best and refuse to nurture any animosity towards them. Hatred will only do you harm and no good. Sit down and plan the way forward without this person in your life. Every time negative thoughts arise in your mind, you must replace them with positive sentiments concerning the person. Worry and stress would be greatly reduced as a result. You may say, but that is not easy to do. Yes, it is not easy, but it is not impossible either. You will be surprised to find out that it is not as difficult as you thought, once you try.

So, buckle up, and chew on the information that follows. Then digest it slowly and implement it into your life as part of your everyday living. What were problems for you will be no longer. Others will marvel at how well you handle situations. Just be generous and let them know where to buy a copy of this book. You may be saving their life.

What Is a Diamond?

Diamonds are beautiful, very hard and costly, precious stones. Diamonds become like this due to the extreme pressure which they undergo. This is quite interesting because when we go through horrible problems, or we are placed under intense pressure, we have the opportunity to become very hard and beautiful. We can emerge from our difficulties like a diamond. Unfortunately, when some people go through intense problems and challenges, they become hard and ugly, rather than hard and beautiful.

Hard is good. Beautiful is good. Most people can relate immediately to beautiful being good. However, when it comes to a person being hard, opinions vary greatly. Therefore, let me explain why hard is good. When a substance is hard, it has certain qualities: solid, firm, tough, unbreakable or not easily broken, resistant to pressure, impenetrable, among others. These are all excellent qualities.

Therefore, when a person endured hardship and emerged hardened, they should possess a personality with some or all of the above qualities. What they stand for and do not stand for can easily be seen by others. They have been through hardship, and having learned from the experience, are no longer easily broken. Problems that easily broke them before or got the better of them can no longer do that. They are the better for it.

When you come under pressure from someone or something, you do not buckle under pressure anymore. You handle stressful situations with grace and poise. People are surprised at how you respond to pressure. When people try to get under your skin or try to rattle your emotions, you respond with control and precision. That is, you are now impenetrable. You are no longer thrown to-and-fro by anyone.

Being hard does not mean being cold. Some people do become hard, but they also become cold. You don't want to oppress others. Being cold usually signifies that there is un-forgivingness, anger, and bitterness bottled up inside of you. If this is so, you can ruin your health and life due to all that stress trapped inside of you.

Some people, a minority, will tell you that everything is always okay. That is because they see the opportunity to improve in every problem or challenge that they face. Most people do not like problems or hardships; however, these hardships have the capacity to help condition you into a better person. Yes, some people indeed become worse as a result. It is not the problems or challenges that they went through that made them bitter and unforgiving, it was their choices and responses. They chose to become like that. Similarly, the person that became better chose to become better despite their circumstances. Notice that both had similar problems and challenges, but their outcomes were different. The difference in outcomes was a result of choice.

That is what being a diamond is all about. It is about taking your experiences, good and bad, and using them to transform yourself into a beautiful and resilient person. You become hard but also beautiful. The hard is necessary.

Benefits of The Diamond Mentality

Every person is a diamond. The problem is, they do not know that they are. A diamond is placed under extremely harsh conditions deep in the earth. Similarly, we are placed under many harsh conditions in life. We are placed under the harshness of deception, lies, un-forgivingness, betrayal, hunger, lack, etc. The pressure from all these issues helps to shape us into diamonds. We all go through some or all of these issues; therefore, we all have the potential to be diamonds. We need to break free from that rock that encircles us and allow the master cutter to expertly cut us so that others will see the beauty in us, the diamond.

A diamond is measured by its four C's. Its carat, clarity, color, and cut.

Carat

Your carats are your heart's capacities. The carat tells the weight or size of the diamond. The more the carats, the bigger the diamond. The bigger the diamond, the rarer and more expensive the diamond. The bigger your heart, the greater your capacity to love, be more compassionate, and be more joyous. Our genuineness comes from our hearts. It has the capacity to love, forgive and show compassion. These are three vital traits in our lives; they help us embrace others regardless of what they have done or who they are. To be able to release those that have done us or our love ones wrong. When we genuinely love and forgive, we can control and get rid of stress quickly; the bigger your capacity to do this, the better.

Clarity

According to *lumeradiamonds.com* virtually all diamonds contain "birthmarks;" these are small imperfections inside the diamond (called inclusions), or on its surface (called blemishes). Clarity refers to the degree to which these imperfections are present. Our clarity then is the degree of our imperfections or faults. The defects in a diamond affect its brilliance. Similarly, our flaws affect how our character shines and positively influence others. How easy it is for people to see who we are. That is, how honest and direct are we so that people do not have to guess about our character. Our lives are an open book.

Color

The less body color in a white diamond, the truer color it will reflect, and the greater its value. For people, true color represents how we interact with and treat other people. Your morals, faith in God, kindness, love, joy, forgiveness etc., are your true colors and give value to you. Your true color is what attracts people to you. The truer colors you have, the more value you have, and the more beautiful you are. As your true colors increase, your body colors will decrease. Sometimes when we meet someone for the first time, we have to wait awhile before they show their true colors.

Cut

Cut does not refer to a diamond's shape (e.g., round, oval, pear, etc.) but to a diamond's proportions, symmetry, and polish. The beauty of a diamond depends more on cut than any other factor. The cut, therefore, represents your upbringing, which has a significant impact on who or what you become. The diamond cutter cuts the diamond in a way that shows its beauty. Our parents brought us up in a way that we can show our beauty to the world. In other words, our parents cut us in a way to make our light shine through easily and beautifully. Initially, your parents cut (mold) you. When you become an adult, you have the power and authority to re-cut (re-mold) yourself. The diamond mentality is a way to help you re-mold yourself so that you reach your fullest potential in all areas of your life. That is, you are well proportioned, symmetrical, and polished.

What does a diamond do? It brings joy to people's lives. Just look at how happy women are when they receive them. Diamonds bring financial security. Their value makes a person feel secure that they have wealth. They add beauty to a person who is adorned with them. When you become a diamond, you will also bring joy, security, and beauty to others.

Do You Need the Diamond Mentality?

If you want a life free of stress or with very little stress, then the answer is yes. If you want to have control over your emotions and be confident about who you are; then the answer is yes. If you desire to be a problem solver, then the answer is yes. However, if you want a life full of stress and sickness, with little or no confidence in yourself, then the answer is no.

Most people desire a stress-free life that exudes confidence. Therefore, this book is for you. *The Diamond Mentality* equips you with all the tools you will need to succeed. It puts you in control of you.

Chapter 2
Can I Buy the Diamond Mentality?

Now you know what the diamond mentality is and its power to transform your life from worry to victory. I am sure you may be asking yourself some very important questions, like, *Does it involve some expensive diet? Do you need to take some pricey course? Do you need a university degree? Is it for the rich? Can I purchase it?* The answer to all these is simply no.

The diamond mentality is for everyone who desires a much better life. It's for the rich, the not so rich and the poor. It's for the educated and the not so educated. As long as you desire a better and happier life, and you are willing to commit to making the changes, then you will have success in developing the diamond mentality. It will transform your life forever from worry, stress, and illness to a happy non-stressed life. You will be a great asset to your family and your workplace. So, stop wondering; yes, it is for you.

Some people may already have a severe stress-related illness. They are heavily medicated, and their health continues to spiral downward. It is not too late for you. The diamond mentality will not cure you, but it can turn off the taps through which stress flows into your system. Imagine a 12-ounce glass being slowly filled with a harmful liquid. When the glass becomes full and more liquid is added, it will overflow and wreak havoc. That glass is your life; the toxic liquid is the stress, and when the glass is full, that is the end of your life. Even if your health is really bad at the moment, let's say your glass is 90 percent full. The diamond mentality can stop your glass from being filled any further and prevent your life from being cut short. You are now able to live out and enjoy the fullness of your life.

So, where can I get the diamond mentality? Where can I find it? As you read along, you will find all the information you need to get the diamond mentality and where to locate it. The diamond mentality is very precious, so take care and never lose it after you find it. Once you've found it, your life will never be the same again.

The Road Map

Whenever you are embarking on a journey you have never been on before; it is always best to get a map. The purpose of a map is to provide information, guidance, and direction on the existence and the location of the destination(s).

This book is your road map to the diamond mentality. Just as you will follow a road map to a destination that you never visited, you need to follow and implement the information given in this book. You trust the road map; similarly, you need to trust this book. It will help you to see where you are and where you need to get to. Just diligently follow the path that you are shown, and it won't be long before you have an encounter with the diamond mentality.

Some of us are going through life, and we don't know where we are or who we are. We sometimes do things that even surprise us. We react to situations in a way that is detrimental to our health and we don't realize that is what we are doing.

Our Creator gave us authority over our bodies, over our emotions, and over all our being. We need to embrace this and step into the power that we were given. When we do that, we will stop reacting to situations and start responding to them. We will prepare in advance our minds, our hearts, and our bodies for anything that may come our way each and every day. When we do this, we will not be defeated by situations or people, but instead, we will be victorious.

An army prepares in advance for battle by having the right training; having access to the appropriate weapons and technology. The army doesn't wait for its enemies to attack and then go and get training and buy weapons. No, the army is prepared in advance so that should they be attacked, they are ready to respond decisively and victoriously. That is how you need to be, ready for every situation that comes against you. If you are unprepared, you will undoubtedly fail and be filled with unnecessary stress. So, take this journey seriously and follow the guidelines as you navigate to your destination, the diamond mentality.

What Do I Need to Have?

Passion

One of the things that separate the successful from the not so successful is passion. When you have a passion for something, you go after it with all your energy. Even when you feel drained, you still pursue that thing because your passion will not let you rest. I am sure you remember having a passion for someone who caught your eye. You left no stone unturned or spared no effort in getting to meet that person. Then, you spent many hours thinking about the person and looking for ways to impress them, so they see you in a positive way.

Passion is the driving force behind highly successful people. Many people have dreams, but many of them lack adequate passion, and as a result, they give up quickly at the first obstacle. I encountered numerous obstacles in writing this book, but I did not give up but plowed forward to the end, not to be defeated because of my passion and belief in what I was doing.

"When you have a passion for something, then you tend not only to be better at it, but you work harder at it too," Vera Wang. Your passion is always there inside of you. When you greatly desire to achieve something, that passion awakens and propels you forward to do what is necessary to achieve it. Therefore, you can be passionate about one thing and not be passionate about another. So, you don't need to look for passion. God has blessed each person with it. What you need to learn is how to activate that passion so that it is in your control and not the other way around. That is, you are being controlled by your passion.

The question is very simple. How much do you desire the good life? A life that is happy, healthy, and free of stress. If you have a passion for the good life, then you are already halfway to achieving it. Just implement the six steps in this book and feel the difference from day one.

Notice that I used the word *desire* in the previous paragraph. Some people get confused between desire and passion. Desire is a good thing but not enough. You may desire many things in one day and act on none of them. For example, you may have a desire to eat ice cream, but you may not lift a finger to get that ice cream. However, when that desire becomes intense, you act on it. It is that intense desire that gives you the passion to act. I like this definition by Stephen Pierce, "Desire is to want something." However, "Passion is the refusal to live without something." From that, you can clearly see why you need to have a passion for your dreams because, without that passion, you will not achieve your goals. Passion helps you to turn stumbling blocks into stepping stones that propel you to achieving your dreams.

You need to develop a passion for the good life, not just for money. You can have millions of dollars and still be filled with worries and illnesses. Many pursue money with a passion only to realize that they are still unhappy when they get the money. They have more worries than when they had little or no money. They now have to worry about others wanting to steal it; how to invest it without losing it; their children may want to put an end to them so that they can get their hands on it, and much, much more. Now you see why some millionaires commit suicide.

So many people today focus solely on making money and lots of it. Many succeed in getting that money because of their passion for achieving. They then realize that they are stressed out, full of worries, and are simply not enjoying life. Many millionaires are miserable and dissatisfied with their life. Many of them have illnesses that the doctors cannot cure because the root cause of the illness is stress which goes untreated. In the cases where it is being treated, the individual is still not improving because each and every day they are exposed to the same stressful environments.

Don't misunderstand me; there is nothing wrong with having lots of wealth. That's not what I am saying. However, if you have lots of wealth and don't have the right mentality to cope and handle that wealth and all the responsibilities that come with it, then your wealth can ruin your life instead of enhancing it. With the diamond mentality, you will be equipped to handle both positive and negative aspects that come with much wealth.

Stressful environments are here to stay. You will always find yourself in these types of environments, whether it is in the workplace, home, school, or other places. So, what can you do about these situations? First, recognize your limitations and your strengths, and be sure to focus on your strengths. Focus on what you can do, not on what you cannot do. You cannot change others, and you may not be able to change your environments. However, you can change yourself, and by so doing, you can have a significant impact on your environment in a positive way that can make a difference.

With the diamond mentality, you can have millions and still have the worry-free life; you can have peanuts and still have the worry-free life. The diamond mentality is for everyone, rich or poor; you first need to have a desire, a passion for it and then you will find that the things you need to do to acquire the diamond mentality will become easy. The diamond mentality cannot be bought; it has to be developed with a passion. It is a way of living each and every day. It is said that perseverance seldom fails, and that is true in the pursuit of good things, so be sure that you will not fail when you persevere after the diamond mentality.

Once you start the program don't let anything or anyone distract you from it; don't make excuses for not following through a specific day. You need to practice it every day until it becomes a habit. Once you have accomplished that, the right actions to prevent worry will automatically come. That is when you are living the luxury of the diamond mentality. It requires perseverance, and that is a choice, not an ability.

After acquiring the diamond mentality, you must make it a part of your everyday life. In other words, it must become a way of life for you; otherwise, you can lose it. There are six steps to the diamond mentality, and once you master these steps, you will literally be living a stress-free life. These six steps are: Acceptance; change of attitude; handling criticism; emotional control; positive thinking; and, controlling your tongue.

Focus

Despite having passion, there are still some other tools you will need to ensure your success. Focus is critical, and the lack of it is one of the leading reasons why some people do not accomplish their goals. Some people are naturally easily distracted. They are unable to keep focus for long periods of time. For this group, there is training available that can help them to increase their attention span.

Some people have a problem with focus, not because of their attention span but because of their inability to prioritize effectively. For example, let's say you have a dream to be a hairdresser. You know you need to get training to become a professional hairdresser and open your own salon. Your aunt calls and asks you to manage her coffee shop. You accept the offer and try to manage the coffee shop while pursuing your studies. You quickly realize that it is too much to handle as managing the coffee shop sometimes takes up twelve hours of your day. You end up missing many classes and failing multiple exams. You spend four years before you get the courage to tell your aunt this is not what you want for yourself. Not being focused on your dream has resulted in a delay of over four years.

The above can be very repetitive for some people. As soon as they are out of one distracting situation, another one that seems important comes up. You keep putting your dreams on the back burner to attend to what seems urgent. It is imperative to set timelines for your goals. When something comes up that appears to be crucial, then you should carefully analyze it to truly see its relevance. Ask yourself a few questions: Can someone else do it just as good? Does it have to be done now?

You have to learn to say "no" even to family members. Some people find it very difficult to say "no" and that can be counterproductive to achieving your goals. You must remain focused on your goals if you want to achieve them.

Knowledge and Determination

Without knowledge, you cannot achieve anything. If you want to bake a loaf of bread, you must have the knowledge to know how to bake that bread. If you're going to repair your computer, you must have the knowledge to fix a computer. Simply turning on your television requires you to know how to turn on a TV. This being the first book I wanted to write, I first had to learn about writing a book. Surprisingly, as I sought the knowledge, I realized I already had some of the tools I would need to write a book. I would not have known that if I didn't do my research on writing books. Research helps to increase your knowledge.

To achieve the diamond mentality, you need to equip yourself with the knowledge you will find in this book. Then you need to put that knowledge to work in your life. Yes, it will be difficult sometimes as you will be tempted to handle problems and challenges the old way. You may want to revert to the stressful way as that is what you know and are accustomed to.

This is where determination comes in. You must be determined to plow forward. Determination is easier to use and be at your disposal when you have a passion for what you want to achieve. It helps you to keep focused on what you want to accomplish. Determination is like the blinkers you put on the horse so that it can only see forward and not be distracted by anything on the sideline. Sometimes all it takes is to choose to move forward, then take a deep breath even in the face of difficulty, even when you cannot see the end. Taking that deep breath after making a choice activates your determination, and that pushes you forward to victory.

Reword Your Sentences

As you start the journey to the diamond mentality you will need to change your vocabulary. That doesn't mean you need to go back to school to learn grammar. All that means is that you need to replace negative words that you now think and speak into your life with positive and encouraging words.

You will need to get rid of words and phrases like "can't," "impossible," "I was born that way," and so on. You need to reword your sentences to motivate yourself. You cannot depend on others to inspire you. When difficulty arises, you must say, "I can and I will." You must say, "I can do all things through Christ who strengthens me. I will be victorious."

I am amazed by the number of people I come across regularly that speak negatively about themselves. I was speaking to a lady at my workplace who wanted to become a nurse. She told me she sat the exam and failed at the first attempt and never retook it. I said to her "you only fail when you give up, you should try again." Her response was, "I don't have the brains for it; it is too difficult." There are so many people out there who lack confidence in themselves. All that is needed is for you to change your vocab and believe in yourself. I believe in you, and I know that you can do it. If I can do it, then you can do it too.

Encourage yourself every day with positive words and statements. When you make that a habit, you will be surprised at how easy you push forward in the face of difficulty. Even on the day you just don't feel like making an effort, you will make an effort because you inspire yourself to succeed.

These are what you will need to have as you start your journey to the diamond mentality. This book is your road map, and if you diligently follow the guidelines, you will arrive at your destination and live the life of the diamond mentality. That is a life with little or no stress and managing your environments so that they don't impact you negatively. Instead, you are in the driver's seat and in control of your environment.

Set Doable Goals

Anxiety is a villain that we do not want in our lives. Keep far from anxiety as it will fill you with stress if you allow it to get inside of you. One of the primary sources of anxiety is the "now" mentality. You want everything "now." Although that is understandable, it is also very counter-productive as it fills you with stress as your mind runs ahead of your accomplishments. Whenever you are doing a task or trying to accomplish something, and your results are lagging behind your mind, you get anxious.

To overcome this source of anxiety, you must control your mind so that it does not run ahead of your physical results. A sure way to do this is to break a task down into more manageable bits. When something appears to be big, or you have too many things to do at once, you can start to feel overwhelmed or frustrated. This can cause you to give up on your goals, or become anxious as you are not achieving the results you will like in the time frame that you have set. Let your mind be in sync with your task and not running ahead.

Remember, Rome wasn't built in a day. Therefore, set doable goals when trying to implement the diamond mentality in your life. Breakdown large tasks into small bits so that they are more manageable. In this way, you will have a feeling of accomplishment, and that in itself, will motivate you to continue because you are getting results. Results motivate.

The diamond mentality has six principles, and each of these is about changing a quality within you. Changing a way of doing things that you have been doing for years is not easy. However, it is not impossible. It may seem overwhelming if you attempt to do it all at the same time. It is, therefore, advisable to try one task or step at a time. Wherever possible, break that step into smaller, more manageable sizes. After you have accomplished one bite-size task, then move onto the other. This method will ensure that you successfully implement the diamond mentality in your life and reaping the benefits.

The next chapter will give you all you need to accomplish the first principle. Though the principles are written in a specific order, you do not need to approach them in the order they are written. Start with the one that seems more manageable to you. I will also recommend that before you start the journey to read the book in its entirety first. This will help you to know the full contents of the book, and then you can decide where you want to start. Wishing you a successful journey to the diamond mentality.

Chapter 3

Acceptance

What Is Acceptance?

It is interesting that these six principles, when written in a particular order, spell out the acronym *ACCEPT*. Learning to accept the things we cannot change should never be taken lightly. Not accepting can be a great source of fatigue and stress as we wrestle with what we have no control over and what we cannot change.

There are some things in life that should be simple, but for some reason, they are not. Those who study human behavior try to explain them, but unfortunately, sometimes the explanation only covers a small group. That is the nature of human beings. Sometimes we are so similar, and at the same time, we are so different. For example, Joan takes the same road to work every day. One Tuesday morning, there was an accident on the road she travels. The road was totally blocked. There were alternate routes, but it required Joan to turn around her vehicle. Instead of choosing to take another route, Joan responded by getting out her car and demanded that the two drivers responsible for the blockage remove their vehicles immediately so she could pass.

Joan spent another two hours arguing with the drivers and complaining to whoever would listen. It would have taken Joan half an hour to reach her destination using an alternate road. Instead, she wasted over two hours having unproductive arguments. Why didn't she just "agree with herself" that there was nothing she could do to resolve the situation. Time is money, and she wasted a lot of time that morning. Joan mishandled that situation, and as a result, she had a terrible headache due to the stress and anxiety from the situation she encountered on the road. This spilled onto her family when she returned home later that evening. Joan didn't have enough energy for them; the stress had drained her. It could have been all avoided if she had just accepted (i.e., agree with herself) that the road was blocked and there was nothing she could do about it.

Acceptance is one of those things that many people have difficulty with. The word in itself has many meanings. I will look only at the definitions that are within the scope of this book. So, what is acceptance?

According to the *Oxford* dictionary, acceptance is: *1. willingness to tolerate a difficult or unpleasant situation. 2. agreement with or belief in an idea, opinion, or explanation. 3. the action or process of being received as adequate or suitable.* Of course, there are other definitions for acceptance.

According to Wikipedia.org, acceptance, in human psychology, is a person's assent to the reality of a situation, recognizing a process or condition (often a negative or uncomfortable situation) without attempting to change it or protest it.

What Are Stress and Anxiety?

Some people may think that stress and anxiety are the same things. Stress and anxiety are different. According to *WebMD* (https://www.webmd.com/balance/stress-management/rm-quiz-stress-anxiety) stress is your response to a change in your environment, be it positive or negative. Your body reacts to change—falling in love, starting a new job, or suffering an unexpected loss—with physical, mental, and emotional responses. However, anxiety is an emotion that is characterized by a feeling of apprehension, nervousness, or fear. Anxiety manifests itself in multiple ways and does not discriminate by age, gender, or race.

Excessive Worrying and Stress

Most research has agreed that chronic worry and emotional stress can trigger a host of health problems. According to *WebMD*, the problem occurs when "fight or flight" is triggered daily due to excessive worrying and anxiety.

You may ask, so, what is "flight or fight?" According to the CMHC (Counselling and Mental Health Clinic), the term "fight or flight" describes a mechanism in the body that enables humans and animals to mobilize a lot of energy rapidly in order to cope with threats to survival.

According to *WebMD*, "The "fight or flight" response causes the body's sympathetic nervous system to release stress hormones such as cortisol. These hormones also boost blood sugar levels and triglycerides (blood fats) that can be used by the body for fuel. The hormones also cause physical problems such as:

Difficulty swallowing	Dizziness
Dry mouth	Fast heartbeat
Fatigue	Headaches
Inability to concentrate	Irritability
Muscle aches	Muscle tension
Nausea	Nervous energy
Rapid breathing	Shortness of breath
Sweating	Trembling and twitching

"When the excessive fuel in the blood isn't used for physical activities, the chronic anxiety, and outpouring of stress hormones can have serious physical consequences on our health, including:

Suppression of the immune system
Digestive disorders
Muscle tension
Short-term memory loss
Premature coronary artery disease
Heart attack

"If excessive worrying and high anxiety go untreated, they can lead to depression and even suicidal thoughts.

"*WebMD* goes on to state that although these effects are a response to stress, stress is simply the trigger. Whether or not you become ill depends on how you handle stress. That is the purpose of the diamond mentality. It does not prevent stressful situations from occurring; It teaches you how to control and manage stressful situations in such a way that your health is not affected. *WebMD* states that physical responses to stress involve your immune system, heart and blood vessels, and how certain glands in your body secrete hormones. These hormones help to regulate various functions in your body, such as brain function and nerve impulses.

"All of these bodily functions and organs interact with each other and are greatly influenced by the manner in which you respond to the various situations you encounter daily. Remember, it isn't the stressful situations that affect your health but your responses, such as excessive worrying and anxiety to the stressful situations. Many people react to stressful situations in a way that may bring on physical and mental illness. We are the masters of life's situations and not the other way around. You can therefore develop the right attitude to these stressful situations and eliminate harmful stress from your life."

Why Don't We Accept Things?

"God grant me the serenity to *accept* the things I cannot change; courage to change the things I can, and wisdom to know the difference."

This prayer, attributed to the American theologian and writer Reinhold Niebuhr (1892-1971), is a very powerful prayer and touches on the importance of accepting the things we cannot change.

For some reason, it is in our nature to struggle. We struggle with our loved ones, we struggle with strangers, we struggle with the institutions, and we struggle with ourselves. We even grapple with things that will have no impact on us. As a result, we cause stress to build up in our bodies. We contribute to our own ill-health. That need not be so. Why can't some people just accept the things that they cannot change?

Most people like to be in a comfort zone. When that comfort zone is disturbed by change, we come against that change. We resist the change. Even when the change is for our good, we still oppose it. For some people, change requires effort to adjust or adapt to the new way. There are many reasons why people resist change. Three prominent reasons are it disrupts our comfort, it requires effort, and fear.

I remember when computers were introduced to workplaces in Barbados in the early 90s, there were many people who resisted the computerization of their workplaces and unions were called in. Two things were happening simultaneously. People's comfort zones were being disrupted and fear of job loss. Employees had to undergo training so they could continue to carry out their functions competently with the new technology. Others feared losing their jobs when the business became fully computerized. Interestingly, most of these people now find it difficult to exist without the computer.

Change can sometimes be painful, and it is understandable why some people find it difficult to accept this type of change. The death of a loved one or the failure of an investment are two examples of painful change.

When my grandmother died, that was very painful for me as we were very close. I had to accept her death and adapt to the new change of life without her. I have never lost a major investment, but I have heard about people who did. This can be so painful for some that they commit suicide.

These are just a few of the reasons why people find it difficult to accept change. Other areas such as marriage, divorce, moving from one location to another, changing a job, building a new home, pregnancy, and many others can result in change and cause stress in our lives; hence some people resist them.

Benefits of Accepting Change

Why is it important for us to accept? What does it have to do with the diamond mentality? Remember, this is only one of six steps that you need to cultivate in your life on a daily basis. Not accepting certain things can have a profound effect on your health. Not accepting can trigger chronic worry and anxiety.

Not accepting causes us to struggle with others, with institutions, and with ourselves. The effort and energy that we dissipate when we fight against things that we cannot change could be used for something more beneficial. In other words, at the end of your struggle with something you cannot change, the process, problem or situation will remain unchanged. All of that energy was for nothing. By accepting, you save energy; you eliminate anxiety and needless worry from your life.

Situations arise in all areas of our lives. Some are agreeable, and some are disagreeable. In most cases, it is the disagreeable ones that cause the stressful situations to arise. These adverse situations can arise in the family, among friends, at work, school, church, sports, social clubs, and others.

Divorces happen because of adverse situations that developed over time or suddenly. Churches split for differences of opinions and behaviors. Friendships are broken due to lack of respect, differences of opinions, taking each other for granted, etc. These and other situations permeate the various institutions in our society, causing problems and challenges to arise. Some of which could have been easily avoided if we had accepted the other point of view. If we had learned when to let go. It doesn't have to be our way or the highway. In many cases accepting or not accepting would not have made a difference. By accepting in many of these circumstances, you may have received joy, happiness, and peace in place of anger, anxiety, and worry, which would have resulted in stress and restless sleep.

Anxiety occurs naturally under stressful conditions. That is perfectly normal. Not accepting the things we cannot change causes us to be stressed. Stress causes anxiety and fear. In *Philippians 4:6*, it is said that we should be anxious for nothing. In the USA, anxiety disorders affect nearly 40 million adults. Research has shown that anxiety produces stress hormones. These stress hormones have very harmful effects on the body and cause a variety of sicknesses, some fatal and others discomforting.

How can you not be anxious in this world that we live in where there is no guarantee? In the next five minutes, you may become ill; your spouse may break the news that they are leaving you; the boss may tell you that your services are no longer needed, and the list goes on. How then can you not be anxious or have fear?

For most of us, when something happens or goes wrong or contrary to our expectations, we want to react to it and change it to our liking, to our way. When we realize that we are unable to achieve this, we get upset, angry, or frustrated. This brings about stress in our lives.

We need to recognize and accept that we cannot fix everything. Neither can we get everything to our liking. We need to learn how to let go, and the first step in learning to let go is to accept. You need to accept that there is nothing you can do about the situation. That being upset isn't going to change anything. Accept that being angry will not cause the problem to vanish, and that getting frustrated will not change the attitude of others.

I know of a lady named Rosalie, whose husband died in a car crash. She found it difficult to accept his death and mourned for him daily. In less than six months, she being grief-stricken, also died. It is alright to grieve for our loved ones, but we should accept that death is a normal part of living. By accepting this is a normal part of living, we can better handle it, when it happens to our loved ones.

To get started creating this awesome mentality, that will transform your personality, first learn to accept what you cannot change. The single most important thing is to accept that worrying will never change or correct anything for the better, that you have done or that was done to you. It is a fact that worrying will increase your stress, resulting in ill-health and added problems. You need to cultivate a behavior of acceptance. Anything that has already happened is in the past, and it cannot be changed, so let it go. When you accept what has happened and recognize that there isn't anything that you can do to change it, but rather there is something that you can do to prevent it from reoccurring in the future; then, worrying is greatly diminished. You can use the experience and knowledge gathered from it to learn for the future and help others.

It is important to note that acceptance doesn't mean doing nothing about the problem or situation; on the contrary. Your decision-making becomes better, more accurate, and faster. You can experience joy and happiness alongside your problems. This single act can reduce your stress levels by approximately 25 percent. No longer will you be banging your head against the wall. No longer will you take problems to bed, allowing them to get between you and your partner. That is one of the reasons why partners find it difficult to communicate effectively in bed. They are in bed, but their minds are on the workplace's problems or on the project.

Accepting does not mean not grieving; however, when you acknowledge that you cannot change what has happened, the mourning period becomes much shorter, giving you more time to look for a solution. So, you see you are doing something but not just anything. You are now focused on solutions that make the situation better. You are now a much better leader in the home, at work, or wherever you may be. It may begin to seem like you are having fewer problems. However, that is not so. It is that you are no longer making an issue out of things that you cannot change. It is because you are now ready with a solution. A problem is only a problem when there is no solution. If there is a solution, then there is no problem.

For example, while working as part of a team on a project, I made an error. The person who saw the error showed it to another team member instead of bringing it to my attention. There were five of us on the team. The mistake was not brought to the supervisor's attention either; instead, they began to secretly talk among themselves about the error. I did not know until Bobby decided to say something about it in a derogatory manner. He did not seek to bring it to my attention in a helpful way. He spoke in a very negative and condescending tone about the error. After a while, because he just kept repeating himself, I interrupted him and acknowledged that I understood; I needed to be more careful and will do everything possible to make sure the error does not occur again.

Despite saying that, Bobby continued carrying on and on about the error. I chose not to allow his comments to affect me but to learn from the situation and put things in place to make sure that it never happens again. What was interesting was that Bobby appeared as if he would explode. I thought that we would have to call the emergency service for him at any moment, he looked like he was going to have a heart attack. Had he known about the diamond mentality, he would have avoided the stress and the possible reduction of his lifetime. I am sure that he reduced his life by about two years by the way he carried on.

From the above example, note that Bobby did not accept that the error had already occurred and that talking about it continuously could not change anything. After nearly an hour, he did not provide a solution to prevent the error from happening again. However, his reaction would have caused his stress level to increase greatly. On the other hand, I accepted that I made an error. There was nothing I could do at that stage to prevent the error. It had already happened. I, however, realized that I could prevent or minimize future mistakes like that from occurring. This would reduce stress on the employees, and the business place would also benefit. When a solution is put in place to prevent an error from reoccurring, it saves the company thousands and, in some cases, millions of dollars. Mistakes can be very costly to a company.

Just hearing or telling yourself that worrying isn't going to change anything is not good enough. From time to time, the challenge would enter your mind or someone may say something to remind you of the issue. Worrying may start again, if only for a short period. However, when you change your attitude about worrying, you will realize that when challenges occur, the time spent worrying is very little or none at all. The response with a solution would be quick and with little or no time wastage. When you start responding to problems or crises in this manner, then you know that you are on the road to having the diamond mentality and becoming worry-free.

How Can I Learn to Accept?

You need to have a desire for the good life, a passion for a truly happy life. When you love life with great benefits, a healthy life without the plagues of stress-related illnesses. A desire to feel energized at the end of the workday so that you have more than enough energy for your family. When you desire a life like that, you will be motivated to accept the things you have no control over.

What's also important is that you understand that you are a work in progress. You are not finished, and you will not be finished. I have come across many people who believe that they have "arrived." One lady said to me, "I will never change, I am perfect." It was interesting when she said that because she was the consummate fault finder constantly complaining about everything. She could always find the smallest of faults when big lovely things were before her eyes. She had severe stress-related health issues such as vertigo, heart disease, and high blood pressure.

Research has shown that vertigo can be triggered by stress and anxiety. Heart-related illnesses can also be triggered or made worse by stress, and high blood pressure can be elevated by stress. It is interesting that a person will refuse to change and think that their way is perfect. Yet, their actions and ways of thinking are contributing to their ill-health.

You are learning to accept when you stop struggling both physically and mentally. You begin to allow. Acceptance is allowing. You can't stop problems from coming your way, but you can turn those problems into opportunities.

Learning to Accept—7 steps to help you learn to accept

You can think of this whole process like one in which a person needs to go to the gym, either to lose weight or to build muscle. You are told "no pain, no gain." Similarly, you can use that phrase here. When you are getting discouraged, remember, "no pain, no gain." So here goes as you begin your journey to the diamond mentality by learning how to accept:

Step 1

Let God Guide You

Let God guide and help you through the process. When you have God in your life, you are able to achieve the extraordinary with less effort. Tasks that seem difficult or impossible are made easy with God. He can give you control where you had no control. He can strengthen you where you are weak. I know that not everyone believes in God, but I would not be honest if I didn't state this as your first step. God has done great miracles in my life. He has strengthened me when I was weak. He has healed me where I was sick. He has increased my finances when I was broke. He has dealt with my enemies when they rose up against me. He has given me hope, joy, and happiness for all to see. He prepared a table before me so that my enemies can see His blessings in my life.

Step 2

Be Honest with Yourself and Check Your Motives

Ask yourself a series of questions. Why am I resisting the change? Would fighting or resisting the thing make a difference to me or anyone else? Is there anything to be gain or lose by opposing? Would prolonging the argument change or accomplish anything? If your answer to any of these questions, except the first, is no, then simply accept because there is nothing to achieve. Time is precious, so don't waste it.

Step 3

Stop Trying to Change People

Stop trying to change adults. Accept them or reject them for who they are. There is a false belief that we can change people. Yes, we can change children and influence them greatly but not adults. Adults are usually set in their ways and will only change or pretend to change if it suits them, or there is something to be gained from it. For example, Neil met a lady named Diana. Neil smoked, but Diana didn't like men who smoke.

However, she really liked Neil and told him upfront that if he wanted a relationship with her, then he must quit smoking. Neil desired Diana and agreed to give up smoking so that he could be with her. Some years later, Diana found out that Neil did not give up smoking; he only pretended to do so. He would never smoke at home. He always smoked before he got home and then used a breath freshener to get rid of the cigarette odor. Diana thought she had changed Neil. She had only opened up herself to deception. There are so many stories like this. Some may argue that they know of stories where the person actually changed. When the person actually changed, it wasn't because the other person changed them. It was because there was something to be gained, whether it was tangible or intangible.

Step 4

Stop Trying to Win Every Argument

Step back and allow someone else to receive the praises. Arguments can be a great source of stress. Sometimes the only thing to be gain from winning an argument is a stroke of one's ego. What are you trying to prove? Is it going to help you or someone else? If nothing is to be gained at the end of the argument, then why compromise your health just for an ego trip. For example, I have heard many of my friends getting involved in political disputes. One person agrees with the measures the ruling government has implemented, while the other disagrees. They seriously argue, call each other names, swear at each other, insult each other, and even threaten one another. At the end, both are angry and stressed, and neither of them has accomplished anything. The measures remain in place.

Step 5

Make Your Actions Count

If you can make a difference, then, by all means, stand up and be counted. You don't need to be stressed to make a difference. Once you have the diamond mentality, then you can accept to make a difference and make changes without stressing yourself. Obstacles and disappointments are a normal part of life. How you choose to respond to these are your choices. It is your response that will determine the level of stress, if any, that you will get.

Step 6

Be in Control of Your Environment and Situations

You need to manage your environment. Many people will try to control us and manipulate us for their own benefit. How you respond to them determines if they will be successful. Remember that when a person tries to manipulate you, they are in fact, trying to control your situation and your environment. You have the right to stop that from happening. When you prevent others from controlling you, you are actually managing your situation, and it's up to you to control or prevent stress from invading you. It is beneficial to you to manage your environment. You are responsible for your environment, and if you don't accept that responsibility, then someone will accept it for you and determine your outcomes. That can be very stressful and detrimental to you.

Step 7

Focus Your Energy on the Things That Matter

Recognize the things in life that you cannot change and accept that you cannot change them no matter what you do. Accepting doesn't mean surrendering. It simply means that you understand that no amount of brainpower or physical power will make a difference. Therefore, it is wise to channel your energy and resources where it matters. I have come across a mindset that believes that worrying means you care. While this may be true in some cases, it is not true in all. Worrying is a natural default response for some people. It is usually as a result of fear or helplessness, and those persons naturally interpret it as caring.

Now that you know these seven steps, all you need to do is to implement them in your everyday life. It will not be easy at first. However, it will become easier as you put them to practice each and every day. The diamond mentality is a way of life, not just something to do once or twice. You will see a great benefit as you live it. Others will be amazed at your positive change and will ask you how do you do it? Just as I didn't keep it a secret from you. Tell them where to buy a copy of this book or better still buy them a copy as a gift. Everyone should own a copy.

How Can Accepting Reduce or Eliminate My Stress Level

You will begin to live the diamond life as you accept other's points of view. No headaches, or worry, due to needless arguments that will accomplish nothing. Having peace of mind because you are in control of your environment, and you are no longer at the mercy of manipulators.

You are using your time to make a positive difference, standing up, and being counted where it matters. In other words, you are making a positive difference in people's lives. That gives you self-satisfaction knowing that your actions are helping others and not wasted on arguments that would accomplish nothing.

Reduce strain on your life and your heart by accepting that you cannot change anyone. Do not beat yourself over your head because someone would not heed your advice and their life continue to spiral downwards. Recognize that our role is to give information or advice, but it is the person's role to accept it to make a difference in their lives. You can force a horse to the river, but you cannot make it drink. Be cautious in giving unsolicited advice. Finally, you will have

total peace of mind when you put God in control of your
life.

Chapter 4
Change of Attitude

While you were growing up, you would have heard both positive and negative comments about the attitude. From the comments you heard, you may have also realized that a person can have different attitudes. I am sure you have heard people say, "She has a very positive attitude" or "He has a very bad attitude." Bearing in mind that those comments are subjective, you may have wondered, what exactly is an attitude?

According to *Merriam Webster* dictionary, the attitude is *the way you think and feel about someone or something* and *a feeling or way of thinking that affects a person's behavior.*

A psychological definition of an attitude is *a relatively enduring organization of beliefs, feelings, and behavioral tendencies towards socially significant objects, groups, events or symbols.* (Hogg, & Vaughan 2005, p. 150)

Your attitude, contrary to popular belief, is not one thing that covers everything. Every person has a number of attitudes. For example, John can have a good attitude towards studying for exams, but a lousy attitude towards exercising. Therefore, when a person compliments or bashes your attitude, they are most likely referring to one particular area.

Your attitudes affect your behavior. The stronger the attitude, the more likely it is to influence your behavior. For example, some people have a positive attitude towards good health. Their behavior is influenced by that attitude therefore you will see that person eating healthier and exercising more. If the person's attitude towards good health was minimal, then that person's actions may not be influenced. They may not go the extra mile to eat healthily and exercise more.

What is a Good Attitude—Having the right attitude?

Your attitude is critical to achieving the diamond mentality, and if you already have a good attitude in general, you are well on the way to the diamond mentality. So, what is a good attitude? A good attitude is encouraging, uplifting, positive, affects others positively, contributes to success, exudes happiness; you are happy for others, smiling even when you are in the midst of challenges, getting up when you fall, not a complainer, not a gossiper, friendly to those you don't know, not allowing your circumstances to dictate your reality, solutions-driven, optimistic, motivated, confident. These are just some of the traits of a good attitude. A good attitude is a great asset to you in your personal and professional life.

An essential part of the journey to the diamond mentality is having the right attitude. You can have a bad attitude or a good attitude towards different things. Most people have mixed attitudes. That is, you may have a good attitude towards work, but then may have a bad attitude towards men or women. To have the right mentality towards all things, you have to be deliberate and purposeful. You have to make the choice to have a positive attitude in general.

People often ask me why I am always happy. I simply tell them I make a choice every day to be happy. Society has taught us that if we have a problem, then we cannot be happy. I had a discussion with a lady from Ethiopia some years ago. She asked a very important question. She asked, "How can a person be happy when they do not have enough to eat?"

I told her, "By being thankful and contented." It is true that it is difficult when you don't have enough. However, being thankful and contented can make a small meal fulling and nourishing. It can put that spark of happiness in you. On the other hand, greed and ungratefulness can make even a big meal appear to be insufficient. I have seen very poor people who are happy and rich people who are sad. I have also seen wealthy people who are delighted, and impoverished people who are miserable. Being content where you are will bring you happiness. Being contented doesn't mean doing nothing about your situation.

You don't need steak and lobster to be happy or to be full. If all you have to eat is rice or vegetables, then eat it with thanks and contentment. You will be full, happy, and more nourished than the person who has the steak and lobster without thanks and contentment. Proverbs 15:17 (NLT) states, *A bowl of vegetables with someone you love is better than steak with someone you hate.* Not being contented adds unnecessary stress to our lives, which affects our health. Haven't you noticed that some people still suffer from ill-health despite the expensive foods that they eat?

With the diamond mentality, you will have a good attitude towards everything. Even when you are faced with problems, you will have a good attitude towards them because you can turn your challenges into opportunities. Every problem presents you with a good learning opportunity. Having the right attitude is really having a good attitude, as outlined above, and applying it daily to every area of your life. The good thing about a good attitude is that it can be created.

You can change your current attitude to a good one if it is not a good one. You have the power to adjust it to give you the rewarding results that you desire, and it is not as difficult as you may think. When you fully understand the power of a positive attitude, you will embrace this quote by Zig Ziglar, "It is not your aptitude but your attitude that determines your altitude."

It is the power of a positive attitude that makes a difference in people's life. That is one of the reasons why two persons will graduate from university with similar qualifications, and one will struggle to make it in his profession while the other will sky-rocket to the CEO position in very little time. Don't knock it until you try it; after all, you have everything to gain and nothing to lose.

Benefits of a Positive Attitude

Your attitude carries a lot of weight in life. Your good attitudes can get you promoted at the workplace; it can get you elected to political office; you can get pardoned or forgiven for a wrong done because of your attitude and get free passes to events and much more. A positive attitude helps you solve problems and inject happiness and enthusiasm into other people's lives. A good attitude reduces stress significantly, thereby reducing or preventing stress-related illness. So, you see the importance and the benefits of a good and positive attitude. It can help you to advance. On the other hand, a bad or negative attitude can be a significant stumbling block to your progress and advancement.

A very important benefit of a positive attitude is "not worrying." When you are free of worry, your mind becomes free to be more creative and to expand. That means, you can grow your business easier because of the new and creative ideas you have. If you are employed, you can bring bigger and better creative ideas to the table, making you an asset to the company. Good news, you don't need to attend university to acquire a good attitude. Neither do you need to be rich to afford a good attitude. All you need to do is choose to have a good attitude.

Have you ever noticed how people that worry about everything age? They always tend to look older earlier than their peers. People who worry also tend to be more prone to ill-health. According to a study published in the *Proceedings of the National Academy of Sciences* journal, negative brain activity is linked with a weakened immune system. The American Heart Association links anger and depression to heart disease and has found it necessary to advise heart attack victims to avoid depression because it could slow their recovery, as well as increase their future risk of heart problems. It is easy to see why one of the health-related benefits of a positive attitude is a healthy heart. A good and positive attitude which reduces stress is also linked to longevity according to the AARP (American Association of Retired Persons).

Another major benefit of a positive attitude is that it boosts your self-confidence. When you have more self-confidence, you feel better about yourself. As a result, you have much higher self-esteem. Low self-esteem is a problem for those with bad or negative attitudes. I know people who are educated to the master's level and still have low self-esteem. Hence, I say again, "It is not your aptitude but your attitude that determines your altitude." These very well-educated individuals help to hammer home the point that it is a positive attitude that contributes significantly to good physical and mental health, creativity, high self-esteem, and much greater benefits.

An interesting benefit of a positive attitude that you may not hear much about is increased energy. Yes, a positive attitude will boost your energy, according to research. Sounds strange but very true. I once worked with a guy named Ronald who had well-built muscles from working out in the gym. He was big, tough, and strong. I, on the other hand, am slim. It was interesting to note that many times, this guy would tell me he was exhausted. Sometimes he would say he didn't feel he could make it to the end of the workday. Our jobs were similar. Regardless of the challenges I had on the job, I still had lots of energy during the day and at the end of the day to participate in other after-work activities like speaking at the Toastmasters' Club.

My energy level had little or nothing to do with my diet. My workmates always complained to me about what I ate. They would say to me, "Hey, Tyrone, you are always eating junk; why don't you get some good food to eat?"

I can also compare because I didn't always have the diamond mentality. Prior to having the diamond mentality, I handled stress very badly, and my attitude wasn't the best. I usually felt drained at the end of the day, and had no energy at all. After work, I had to go home and take a nap immediately to get back a little energy before I could do anything. Now I am older with a diamond attitude, and I am much more energetic at the end of the day. Stress drains you of your energy and leaves you weakened. A positive attitude does the opposite, and your energy is replenished multiple times in a day.

I love this quote so I will share it with you because it is so true. "A positive attitude may not solve all your problems, but it will annoy enough people to make it worth the effort," Herm Albright, quoted in *Reader's Digest*, June 1995.

By coincidence, I realized that when people are trying to annoy you or get you mad, just respond positively. For some reason, that gets them angry. It isn't that you want to make them irritated; you just don't wish to lower your standards. If you cannot find something positive to say and you love music, just sing a song. Yes, happily sing and smile, which will have a similar effect while helping you control your emotions. What they were planning for you is turned on their heads, and you have come through it all stress-free. That's the power of a positive attitude and positive words.

When you have a positive attitude, you become more confident. This, in turn, improves your self-esteem, and you begin to believe in yourself. This can propel you to achieve your goals faster. You are happy to spend time with yourself as a result of your positive attitude, which gets rid of loneliness. Studies show that people who feel lonely are more prone to depression and sadness. Being alone or living alone does not make you feel lonely. You can be in a house full of people and still feel lonely.

Impact of Your Choices on Your Outcomes

Worrying can have a negative effect on your attitude, and a positive attitude is worry's greatest nightmare. You need to develop an attitude of looking for the positive in people and things, always being grateful and optimistic. With the right attitude, you will be able to bounce back quickly and nip worrying in the bud. Always remember, you cannot change people, but you can change yourself.

It is said that 90 percent of what happens to you is as a result of your choices and the other 10 percent due to the actions of others. This is very true, and you will see as you read the impact of a positive attitude on your choices and, by extension, your outcomes. Consider this example:

I ordered four items from a popular computer store, and the items were shipped as two separate shipments. The first shipment arrived on the second day as promised by the sales clerk; however, I missed the courier, which meant I had to go to the post office to collect the item the next day. The courier had called, and I was at home but when I got to the phone, it had rung off. I tried calling back, but no one answered.

My mind became flooded with negative thoughts. There was an attempt to worry because of the time it would take to go to the post office the next day to collect the item. However, I nipped those thoughts in the bud. "Worrying" isn't going to get me the parcel, I said to myself. I chose not to worry and focused on what needed to be done to get the package. By so doing, I activated the attitudes of problem solving and encouragement. I needed to encourage myself that if I wanted the parcel, then I must go for it the next day according to the courier's instructions. The next day after 1 pm, as per instruction, I went to the post office and collected the package. I felt really good with myself as I now had the packet in my possession, and I didn't stress over the situation.

The next shipment was not as timely as the first and, to my disappointment, arrived six days later. I had bought this for my daughter and I really didn't want to disappoint her by giving her later than I had promised. I did everything possible not to miss the courier, including keeping my phone next to me so that I could answer it quickly and avoid what happened with the first package, which, by the way, was my son's birthday gift. Wherever I went, including the bathroom, I took the phone with me to avoid missing the courier. I don't usually carry my phone to the bathroom.

I looked at the time, and it was 2 pm. I didn't hear from the courier, and my phone hadn't rung. Negative thoughts tried to invade my mind, but I pushed them away and deployed a positive attitude. This all happened at the time when I was implementing the diamond mentality in my life. I decided to go online to track the package. To my amazement and shock, the tracking information indicated that the courier came at 11:15 am that morning.

My blood began to heat up, but before anger could set in, I chose to adopt an attitude of calm and positivity. Questions came to mind like, *Why didn't he call?* However, I refused to let my mind take control of me. So, I quickly adopted a positive attitude and gave the negative thoughts the "boot." I nipped the propensity to worry in the bud, and told myself that after worrying, I still had to go to the post office tomorrow to collect the item. I accepted that there wasn't anything else I could do to change the situation. Worrying will not achieve anything except a headache.

Around 3:30 pm that same day, I went downstairs to clear my mailbox. To my surprise, the package was in the mailbox. The courier had somehow managed to get the item to fit into the mailbox. I would never have thought that the package could fit into the mailbox. That also meant I would not need to go to the post office the next day.

I then said to myself, *Now you see again why worrying is a waste of time and energy and should always be avoided.* The item is here, so if I had worried, I would have affected my health needlessly. That was a *wow* moment for me.

How to Activate a Positive Attitude?

Choice is one of mankind's greatest gifts. Although choice is not a hot topic in today's society, its importance can easily be seen by people's reactions whenever anyone tries to take their choice away from them. History has shown that people rebel when their choices are taken or restricted. Slaves rebelled and rose up against their masters throughout history. People who are suppressed by an invasion of their country rebel against their captors and carry-out guerrilla warfare. Children rebel against their parents, who try to restrict or control their choices, and the list goes on.

To activate a positive attitude, you must make the choice to do so. That is the root or the most important thing you must do. Why? Because you must be in control of all your being (faculties), whether it be physical, mental, or emotional. Your choices put you in control. For many people, their emotions control them, and as a result, they lack control in their lives. If your emotions are guiding you, then you are not in control. You are being controlled.

We were created to be in control of all our faculties and emotions. A person without control is like a country without a defense. Anyone can invade it. You don't want to be invaded by your emotions. You want to control them. Like the previous example, my emotions attempted to take over when I didn't hear from the courier. I had to use the authority given to me by God to take control of my emotions; otherwise, they would have dictated to me how I should react. All of us were given that authority; all of us don't use it.

Let's say, for example, a fellow worker comes up to you and says, "If this company were mine, you would be fired a long time ago." Your natural instinct is for your emotions to kick in and retaliate. First, you need to control that desire to retaliate; if you're having difficulty doing that, then take about five deep breaths and slowly exhale each one. Next, choose to respond with a positive attitude. You can say something like, "Thank you for your unsolicited opinion; if ever you need a friend, I will be delighted to be your friend." If you find that a positive response is difficult for you in such a situation, just say nothing. Simply ignore the person, and that includes not having internal conversations with yourself. After all, the person's comment does not carry any weight. My grandmother taught me that if you don't have anything good to say, then do not say anything at all.

To help you activate your positive attitude, if you don't naturally have one or to improve on your existing one, try to initiate greetings with those you meet by telling them something complimentary or suggesting to them to do a good deed today. For example, you see a work colleague in the parking lot. You go over and say, "Hello, you are looking great today." You could also say something positive about their clothing, hair, or shoes. Alternatively, you could say to them, "You have a great smile."

Light up every person's life you come into contact with by greeting them with your beautiful smile. Practice this every day until it becomes a natural part of you. Remember, practice makes better.

Six Steps to A Positive Attitude

A positive attitude is necessary for the diamond mentality. These six steps will help you to attain a positive attitude. If you find you have a negative attitude, these six steps will certainly help you get a positive one. If you are somewhat positive and would like to improve, then these steps will also help you. In other words, they are good for everyone.

Step 1

Desire the Good Life

The good life is a life with little or no stress and filled with joy and happiness. LaPiere concluded from his study that the stronger the attitude, the more likely it should affect your behavior. Therefore, if you construct a strong and good attitude towards a good and happy life, it would become easy to develop behaviors to accomplish that. In other words, doing what it takes to create a positive attitude will become easier as long as you have a strong desire for the good life.

Step 2

Fill Yourself with Positive Information

You cannot take something from a container if that container doesn't contain the thing. So, the first thing you need to do is fill yourself with positive words and thoughts. You are the container. Therefore, go online and look for positive quotes to read every day. Even reading one quote per day is better than reading none. Use these quotes in your life to encourage yourself and to encourage others. Also, read other positive motivational material and listen to motivational speeches. In a short time, you will be filled with positive material that will easily flow through and from you. Your conversations will become richer and your responses solution-driven.

Step 3

Don't Take Everything Personally

You cannot change others, but you can change yourself. Every attack on you is not about you. Sometimes, the attacker is just having a bad day or unloading some of their garbage, and you happened to be there. You'll be surprised at the amount of garbage some people are carrying around. Therefore, you don't need to respond to every negative that someone says or does. If you must respond, then do it positively, drawing from the positives you have been reading and listening to. Ignoring is also a positive response when used against negativity.

Step 4

Control Your Emotions

This is a big one and is dealt with in detail in that chapter. Emotional outburst wreaks a lot of havoc in people's lives. All persons involved suffer as a result. The lack of emotional control is so big that it sometimes results in the loss of life, incarceration, and damage in many forms. That is why it is essential to control it. When you are able to control your emotions, you are definitely in the driver's seat to changing your attitude to a positive one.

Step 5

See Problems as Challenges and Not as Stumbling Blocks

When you see problems as challenges, you are more driven to find a solution. You become solution-focused rather than problem-focused. You become excited, instead of stressed at the thought, of finding a solution for the challenge, or to overcome the challenge. You recognized that every challenge brings with it something new to learn. Therefore, challenges are also an opportunity to increase your knowledge base.

Step 6

Replace Your Negative Vocab with Positive Ones

Instead of saying, "I can't," you'll now say "I can." Instead of saying, "I have to go to work," which can make work feel so burdensome and stressful. You will now say "I get to go to work." All the "have to" in your life can now be replaced with "I get to." Making positive and motivating statements not only encourage you but they also inspire others.

After you have implemented these six steps in your life, you will have a really wonderful attitude. For some people, when they see a small molehill, they cry out, look, that's a mountain. For the person with the right attitude, when they see a mountain, they say, *look there's an opportunity*. Now that you have all you need to change your attitude to the right attitude, you will soon be seeing the mountains in your life as opportunities. Opportunities for growth; opportunities for cultivating new relationships; opportunities for learning; opportunities for being more creative, and much more.

It is interesting that when we are thrown into a problem, it will either make us or break us. When it makes us, it means we came up with solutions or someone helped us out of the situation. We had no choice but to find a solution or seek help if we couldn't, in order to survive. Unfortunately, when the dire situation was over, we were so glad to get out of it that we didn't even want to think about it anymore than was necessary. We put it behind us and moved on, and in a short time, we forgot how we dealt with that bad situation.

A couple months later, or a few years later, you are faced with a big problem, and you react similarly with panic. It is as if this is the first time you are faced with a crisis. You forgot you had solved a similar problem a few years before. You also forgot how you solved that problem. When you deliberately change your attitude instead of circumstances changing it, you will remember the strategy you used or you implemented to solve previous challenges. You will then be able to use these strategies for any future challenges. What does that mean? It means that future problems will not be burdensome and stressful. You will not suffer from anxiety, and as a result, you will have a more joyful life.

The right attitude is necessary. However, to have the diamond mentality you need more than the right attitude. You are on the right path so continue to the next chapter and learn the importance of handling any type of criticism.

Chapter 5
Criticism – Learn to Handle It

What is Criticism?

Some people have great out-going personalities while others are more reserved and private. However, there is something in life that does not discriminate who will get it. You will get it regardless of who you are or where you are from. Whether you ask for it or not or whether you're going to welcome it, you will receive it. Sometimes it is boldly given to you, right up in your face, and at other times you're not aware you are getting it because it's given to you from behind your back. That thing that we all get, like it or not, fair or unfair, welcome or unwelcome is criticism.

According to *oxforddictionaries.com,* criticism is, *1. The expression of disapproval of someone or something on the basis of perceived faults or mistakes. 2. The analysis and judgment of the merits and faults of a literary or artistic work.*

Criticism is often seen as negative, but that is not always the case. Criticism can also be positive. Many people now opt for the word "feedback" as this tends to have a more positive impact on people. Feedback tends to guide people into giving both positive (constructive) and negative (destructive) criticism, but in a way, that is encouraging and motivating.

Different Types of Criticism—Constructive vs Destructive

You have probably heard of constructive criticism and destructive criticism, and you have probably received both. Constructive criticism is given with the intentions of helping the person being criticized to improve or to motivate them to do better. Destructive criticism is where the criticizer's intention is to put you down and make you feel insecure. As mentioned before, life is about how you react or respond to it. It doesn't force you to react, or tell you how to respond. Why did I say that again? With the diamond mentality, it doesn't matter what the intentions of the criticizer are. What matters is how you take the criticism and respond to it. You will improve and learn from criticism of any type providing you respond correctly. You will learn how to handle all types of criticism. Therefore, if someone should give you unsolicited destructive criticism, you will be able to use it to your advantage and overall improvement.

Even before I knew anything about the diamond mentality, I remembered I always had a passion to improve on my life. As a result of that desire, I welcomed criticism of every type and from anyone. I knew that no matter the intentions of the criticizer, I would be able to find something in the criticism that would help me to improve. Therefore, I sought out people I knew who were bold and would say it like it is with no concern for my feelings. As my grandmother used to tell me, "…because someone call you a fool doesn't make you one."

Some of the criticism I received was constructive and some was destructive. I worked as an economist for the government. In my early years, I had to write many reports. I knew that my writing was not as good as it should be, and so I always asked for criticism of my work so that I could improve. The best criticism I received came from my supervisor Dr. Layne, whose English was impeccable. Dr. Layne would call me into his office and point out the errors I had made and suggest how I could avoid them in the future. Even when there were no errors, but the report could be made more interesting, he would highlight those areas to me. He would never criticize my work in front of others.

However, the way he delivered the criticism was gut-wrenching. He didn't put it over nicely, or at least I didn't think so. Initially, when he first came to the office, I was taken aback and thought, why is this man picking on me? I quickly told myself not to take it personally but to look at what he said objectively and try to improve. I did that, and soon my work was improving. The criticism from him got less and was replaced with compliments. Though he came over as harsh, his intentions were good. His aim was to help me to improve, and he succeeded. That is constructive criticism. It helps you to become better at whatever you were doing, providing that you respond the right way.

When I was less than eight years old, my grandfather bombarded me with destructive criticism. He would tell me the most discouraging things and in the most hurtful ways. I was only a kid, and if I dropped something, I would be called an invalid; told that I couldn't do anything properly.

If I played a lot of games as most boys my age did, I was told I would never amount to anything.

At that age, I certainly didn't know anything about taking negative criticism the right way. However, I had an interesting personality from an early age. Some may say I was born that way. I always had a strong desire to prove wrong those who dared to tell me I couldn't get something done. I had to show them they were wrong about me and set out to prove it. The fact that my grandfather told me I would not amount to anything motivated me to prove to him that I will amount to something. I became a qualified electrician some years after and was quick to let him know.

With destructive criticism, you need to look for the positive. There is positive in everything. You must never become the negative that people say about you. Using the example, I gave earlier, if someone calls you a fool, that doesn't make you one. You decide who you are and what you become. Remember also that many people we interact with on a daily basis are carrying around lots of garbage with them. They will use any excuse to dump their trash on you. Don't be like the pavement and accept the garbage that is dumped on it; instead, reject it.

Later, I took on wine-making as a hobby and gave away bottles of wine with the condition that the tasters or drinkers provide criticism of the wine. Needless to say, I was a natural in this area, and 99 percent of the criticism was so positive, I didn't believe them. I was told by some, there is nothing you need to do the taste is excellent, the alcohol content was potent, the flavor is rich and not watered down. One guy said all you need to do was to make more.

Later, I entered a winemaking competition. The main purpose was to get an unbiased opinion. The culinary arts competition was an annual national competition and was organized so that the competitors could not be identified. I was pleasantly shocked when I won a gold medal. That taught me not to be too hard on myself and that the positive reviews that I had received were true.

I mentioned the above not to boast of my wine-making skills but to demonstrate how we can easily reject criticism that is true, especially when we are exceeding our expectations. Sometimes we are too hard on ourselves, and when people tell us that we are good at what we are doing, we reject it as a lie. On the other hand, sometimes, we overestimate ourselves, and we may receive some "negative" criticism. The criticism may indicate to us that we are not as good as we think, and we should try to improve before moving forward. When we are overconfident, we reject the criticism and the criticizer only to realize later that they were right. Of course, there are other reasons why people may reject criticism. For example, low self-esteem. Whatever the reason, we should always be aware that no matter how horrendous something may sound, we can learn and grow from it. Improving on yourself should never be an option but a daily goal.

Criticism occurs in every area of life. You will find both types of criticism in the workplace, in the church, in social groups, in the home, on the streets, etc. Wherever you go, you will find criticism. There is nothing you can do to get rid of or abolish it. However, you can respond to it in a manner that puts you in control. That way, you remain stress-free and energized. The diamond mentality will equip you with the tools to help you to respond to criticism positively.

How Can Criticism Help the diamond mentality?

We are constantly distracted by many things each and every day. This is a part of life, but we need to filter out the distractions so that we can accomplish much. Some people are more successful than others in filtering out unwanted distractions. For some people, certain types of distractions are addictive, so they find it difficult to filter them out. The television, telephone, tablet, and social media are examples of distractions that can become addictive.

A huge distraction with a high propensity to cause us to worry and become stressed is criticism. As mentioned before, criticism is not always solicited. Many people take it upon themselves to give criticism without being asked. In most cases, the intentions of the people are good. Some gossip could be seen as a form of negative criticism and is very distracting for the gossiper and the targeted persons. For example, after Deborah left the room, Barbara began to gossip about Deborah's hair indicating that she should spend more time on her hair to make it look better. Deborah became aware of what was said about her and made an effort to come to work with her hair well done. Deborah took the negative conversation that took place behind her back to improve on herself.

Unfortunately, many of us are highly sensitive, and criticism can negatively impact our emotions. This effect can be so significant that we can be impacted for days and sometimes longer. This is further compounded by the internal conversations we have with ourselves. These inner conversations can be very damaging to us. In addition to the effects of stress, they can also cause low self-esteem and an inferiority complex. It should be noted that many of the people who give destructive criticism have some form of low self-esteem. When they put down someone, it makes them feel good about themselves.

So, what is "internal conversation" some may be asking? This is simply talking to yourself in your mind instead of out aloud. The danger comes about when you have a conversation on behalf of the person you have the issue with. You answer on behalf of the person, and you take the answer and literally respond in action as if it had really come from the person. For example, after becoming aware that a co-worker tampered with your work, you decided to confront the person. Before that happens, you go through a thought process of what you will tell the person. Part of those thoughts is an assumption of how you think the person would respond. Your mind tells you the person is going to react very negatively, and you believe that. On approaching the person, you verbally attack them without giving them a chance to explain.

Your mind and brain need to get a regular workout if it's to develop into the diamond mentality. It's like a bodybuilder. If he wants to be a first-class body-builder, he must work out regularly in the gym with the various weights, and eat the right foods to contribute to the muscle mass that he desires. Similarly, you must work out your brain and your mentality every day to develop the diamond mentality.

When you encounter criticism daily, you must respond as outlined in this book. Criticism helps you to develop emotional control. Just imagine you are doing your work as usual, and a co-worker comes along and say, "you are always making a mess; you don't seem to be able to get it right." You are now wondering what you did to deserve such a comment. Your brain immediately goes into overdrive to protect you from this person. This triggers your emotions, and you are about to tell off this person in the worse possible way. You have to use every ounce of control to stop your mouth from opening and creating a scene in the workplace.

The first time something like that happens, it will be very difficult to control your emotions and your tongue. However, like the bodybuilder when you practice these steps daily, each one becomes easier and easier until it is like a "piece of cake." Being able to handle criticism helps you control your tongue and develop the ability to ignore potentially volatile situations.

Criticism can help you to control your anger if taken the right way. Just imagine someone says to a person who is easily angered, "You need to control your anger before you get arrested for assaulting someone." The person gives thought to what was said and recognizing that there is truth to the statement because when they get angry, they feel like getting physical with the person they are angry with. The person then responds by making an effort to get help to control their anger. It was the criticism that got them thinking about getting help regardless of the criticizer's intentions.

Some people who are not easily predisposed to anger sometimes actually surprise themselves at their responses to things that other people do or say. I am one of those. I was never a person who was easily angered. I was actually in the process of developing the diamond mentality when this situation occurred. I was doing my job at one of my previous workplaces when suddenly, without warning or invitation, I was verbally attacked by a co-worker. He yelled, "If I was the owner, I would fire you."

My brain and emotions immediately took over, and I reacted in a way that I hadn't in over 20 years. I thought to myself, *I didn't do anything wrong, and neither did he mention anything that I did that was wrong.*

If that guy had come any closer at that moment, I would have punched him.

After the incident, I chastised myself for allowing someone to get me angry. I actually thought I was past that. I knew then I still needed to do more work on myself in that area. I worked on it, and interestingly enough, the same guy verbally attacked me again some weeks later, and I handled it in a way that I felt very good about myself. I was not angry, neither did I lose control at any time. It was a really good feeling. Some months later, that same guy was demoted for his behavior towards another co-worker. Six months later, he was fired. That unwarranted attack had helped me to improve on my diamond mentality. In your pursuit of the diamond mentality, see problems as opportunities; welcome them and use them to improve on yourself. Yes, you may slip-up at some time and revert to your old behavior. Don't be discouraged, don't give up, continue to pursue the diamond mentality, you'll love yourself for it.

Responding to Gossip

Gossip is a past-time for some people, and you should stay far away from it as it can cause you unnecessary worry. It is difficult to understand why so many people like to wallow in gossip each and every day. It is very time-consuming and your time could be better utilized developing strategies to accomplish your goals. Too much time wasted on other people's business means less time spent on yours.

People will say bad and untrue things about you. There is nothing you can do about that. There will always be those who are for you and those who are against you. You have to choose how you will react to such things. A simple response can nip the gossip in the bud. Here is an interesting way to look at gossip targeted at you. Instead of seeing yourself as a victim, see yourself as very important, so important, that others would spend their valuable time talking about you. Don't hesitate to share this outlook with those who gossip about you. That may actually stop them from gossiping about you as their intentions are not to make you feel important or good about yourself. Remember, your response to gossip must never stress you out.

Benefits of Handling Criticism Well

Shalene recently said to me, "You don't care about anything or anyone. I never see you worry about anything. When you care, you worry,"

I responded, "There is no connection between caring and worrying. It is true that people worry about the ones they care for. However, they don't worry because they care. They worry because they fear. Fear causes us to worry. We fear when we don't know what to do to help our loved ones. When our loved ones are making bad choices, we fear they will get hurt. When we don't have a solution to help, we fear." The diamond mentality helps you to get rid of fear.

Then I told her that is why I don't worry. With the diamond mentality, you are solutions driven. You don't waste time gossiping or having conversations that don't help the situation. You focus on finding a solution or finding someone or something that can help you get a solution. Though I cannot say with 100 percent accuracy that my response to Shalene helped her. I can say that I responded well to her criticism. I was not annoyed or angry at any time during the conversation. I have also noticed that Shalene's outbursts at work are much less than before.

Those are two great benefits of handling criticism well. You get rid of fear, and you are solutions driven. You maximize your time because you recognize that time is precious. Positive people like being around you because of how you respond to negative things. Negative people keep their distance from you because they can't believe you are genuine. Life is precious and limited, so you don't waste your time anymore. These are just some of the benefits of being able to handle criticism well, which in turn, contributes to the development of the diamond mentality.

Whenever you are getting constructive criticism or otherwise, accept the criticism and truthfully ask yourself. *Does this apply to me?* By doing this, you will find that no matter the criticism, you will find some part of it to be relevant. Next, ask yourself the question, "What do I need to do to bring about positive change in myself?" Then search yourself to find the relevant answers and implement them in your life. On the other hand, if you get emotional and deny that the criticism is not relevant to you, then you will not benefit from the criticism.

For example, a previous boss of mine called a staff meeting where he mainly talked about things that he didn't like at the office and asked us to try to improve on those things. He sharply criticized an inspector who constantly got to work late every day. He, however, did not mention the name of the inspector, but everyone knew whom he was referring to. It was interesting that after the meeting, we were having a conversation about the meeting. What we called "the meeting about the meeting." To our surprise, when we got to the topic of lateness, the perpetrator stated loudly, "Well, I know he couldn't be referring to me because I get to work early every day."

There was instant silence, and everyone just looked at each other before laughing out loud. Needless to say, the perpetrator continued to get to work late, and there was no change on his part, prompting the boss to take further action against him sometime later. The criticism was not taken, and as a result, there was no change.

When you make an error, some people will criticize you and rake you over the coals. You don't want to have worrying thoughts about the mess you made, the negative things that people are saying about you, and what they think should happen to you as a result. This is when arguments take place, internal conversations take over, frustration kicks in, and sometimes suicide happens if allowed to get out of hand. Try to avoid buying into negative criticism from anyone, including yourself. Yes, we are sometimes very hard on ourselves and criticize ourselves harsher than others, which could negatively impact our progress.

Six (6) Steps That Will Help You to Handle Criticism Well

It's a fact that unwarranted attacks or criticism can activate a reaction that can even surprise you. Some surprises are good, but others can be frightening. Not having control over your reactions can be detrimental to you and/or your career. It is, therefore, important that you are in control of your reactions and responses to destructive criticism and to criticism in general. Here are six steps to help you handle criticism better.

Step 1

Stay Cool

Don't lose your cool! Remain calm. Some words can trigger your emotions, so exercise control and remain calm. That may not be easy for some people, so if you have trouble being calm in awful situations, then try one or more of the following:

A. Admit to yourself that you are angry. When we are honest with ourselves, we are more likely to do something about our challenges than if we are not. Kim, a past workmate was visibly angry with

Marlon. I said to her, "He isn't worth your time and energy, just try to calm down."

She shouted, "I am not angry!" Kim's face and entire demeanor had changed. She was literally shouting, and I could hardly get a word in edgewise. In this situation, Kim did not acknowledge her anger and therefore did not do anything about it but continued to rage.

B. Take deep breaths and exhale very slowly. This normally helps to calm you and put you back in control of your emotions.

C. Count. Yes, count from 1 to 50. If you are still not in control by the time you reach 50, then continue but count backward from 50 to 1.

D. Thank the person for the criticism letting them know that you feel honored that they would take some of their precious time to think of you. Alternatively, you could pay them a compliment.

Step 2

Listen

Listen with an open mind. Remember, you have two ears and one mouth. That means you should listen twice as much as you talk. Control the urge to speak when another is speaking. That way, you can fathom all that the person is saying.

Step 3

Ponder

Ponder on what the person is saying to you. When you do this with an open mind and objectively you will see both the positives and negatives of the person's opinion.

Step 4

Ask the Person to Repeat

This can give you time to collect your thoughts and control your emotions so that your response is positive. Elvis said to Laura, who had not asked for his opinion: "That dress looks bad on you."

Laura, taken aback, replied, "I can't be hearing you right. Could you repeat what you just said."

Elvis bellowed in a loud voice, *"I said your dress looks bad."*

Laura politely replied in a very soft voice, "Thank you, I wasn't aware that you were an expert on fashion."

Step 5

Filter Out the Garbage

Filter the information that you just received and throw out the negatives and keep the positives. Implement the positives into your life to bring about positive growth.

A person may say something negative to you with the worst of intentions. However, you can choose to respond positively and use that situation for positive growth in your life.

Step 6

Be Willing to See Things from the Other Person's Perspective

This could calm the person and cause them to start seeing you as a fair person. Therefore, word your sentences in such a way that they affirm the person and not degrade them.

Opportunities will happen most days to give you a chance to practice and sharpen your skills. Sometimes, you may slip-up and react the way you did in the past. Don't let that discourage you, instead, analyze the situation and plan in advance the appropriate actions to take should a similar situation occur in the future. You are the master of your responses so let each one contribute to your well-being.

Chapter 6
Emotional Control

What is Emotion and being Emotional

We have all experienced some emotion in our lives whether frustration, fear, hatred, love or other emotions. According to *thefreedictionary.com*, emotion is *a mental state that arises spontaneously rather than through conscious effort and is often accompanied by physiological changes; a feeling: the emotions of joy, sorrow, and anger.*

Bing.com defines emotion as *a natural instinctive state of mind deriving from one's circumstances, mood, or relationships with others.*

Sometimes we are told we are getting emotional or stop being emotional. What exactly does it mean to be "getting emotional?" While this is a subjective statement, the person is usually referring to a specific period where the other person has become greatly reactive and appears to be losing control. This state of mind and body can expose the person to greater stress, depression, or anxiety.

Some people may argue that emotion is a good thing, while others may assert it is not. Human beings were created with emotions. That tells me that it is a very good thing.

However, just like every part of your body, you need to control your emotions. Unfortunately, some people think it is acceptable to let go of their emotions. My question to them is, "Do you allow your feet to take you where they please or your hands to take up whatever they like when you go to the department store?" I am sure your answer is no. Like your feet, hands, and other body parts, you should control your emotions. Your emotions are a part of you.

As mentioned before, God created us with emotions; therefore, He should have something to say about them. It also follows that if God created us with emotions and He created us in His image, then God also has emotions. We all will agree that anger is an emotion. In *1 Kings 11:9 (KJV)*, it clearly states that God was angry with Solomon. *2 Kings 17:18* and other scriptures also mentioned God being angry.

Love

I had a friend named Susan who was physically abused by her boyfriend, John. He beat her mercilessly. Her friends advised her to leave him, but she would not. At that time, they were living on the premises of John's employer. Some years later, they decided to build their home. When she told me, I advised her not to do so since the abuse had never stopped. Her sister also advised her against it as well as many friends.

Susan ignored us all and said she loves him and believed he would change. I told her it was now over ten years, and if he hasn't changed yet; it was unlikely that he would change now. As usual, she ignored the advice given and proceeded to join with her boyfriend to build the house.

Some years later, after the house was completed, Susan called to tell me she was in the hospital. Her boyfriend tried to kill her while she was sleeping. He smashed a ceramic lamp on her head and then proceeded to beat her. She was barely able to escape as the neighbors heard the screaming and called the police. She was unconscious when she was taken to the hospital and spent six weeks in the hospital recovering from head injuries and fractured ribs. It took her quite a while to fully recover after being discharged from the hospital. It was then that Susan decided that she will not go back with him.

If Susan were able to control her emotions and look at the facts, she would not have had to endure the torment and pain that she did. One significant fact that many people have a problem accepting is that they cannot change anyone, even a loved one. Change comes from within, and only you can change yourself. No one can do that for you. I understand that we do not like to see our loved ones ruining their lives by making bad choices. However, all we can do is offer guidance in the form of information. It is up to the person as to what they would do with the advice and information. As my adorable grandmother used to say, "You can force a horse to the water, but you cannot make it drink." Similarly, we can force someone to the counselor, but we cannot force them to implement the recommendations into their life. I have seen many individuals trying to change others but ended up ruining their own life. Love is a powerful emotion, and we can control any impulses as a result of it.

Anger

Anger is also a powerful and volatile emotion. It can move you to act impulsively without thinking and cause you to have regret after the anger has subsided. Anger can also fill you with wrath and, even worse, hatred. Some people find it very difficult to control their anger, while others tend to become easily angered at the slightest thing.

As a teenager, I went to a party with a small group of guys. We were having fun dancing and drinking with the girls. We then went over to the bar to rest our feet for a while and engage in some exciting conversation as we usually do. Mark then threw out the question that started the conversation, "What do you guys think about prostitutes?" Everyone laughed, and then Greg volunteered to give the first response. The discussion was interesting, lively, and full of fun until Mark responded to a comment that Greg made that could be interpreted that Greg has a thing for prostitutes. Greg reacted angrily, and his entire demeanor changed. He became more and more agitated and angry. As an exchange of words continued between these two, Greg became louder and louder and point his finger into Mark's face. It wasn't long before he deliberately poked Mark in the face, and the two started to fight. When it was all finished, Mark was left with a fractured nose. Our night was ruined as a result.

Anger is a very controlling emotion, so I recommend that you avoid getting angry rather than think that you can handle it. When you are angry, a single word or action can push you over the edge and cause you to do something that you may regret for as long as you live. When you implement these six strategies into your life, you will be able to control that emotion of anger and save yourself from regret and stress in the long-run.

The Holy Bible also advised us against getting angry. In *Psalm 37:8*, it states, "Refrain from anger and turn from wrath; do not fret; it leads only to evil." From that scripture, you can see that anger can lead to evil if not controlled. Even if you are a nonbeliever, you can see the things that happen around you. You read the news and listen to it on radio and television, and I am sure you have heard of people committing murder because of anger. People become violent and reckless because they were angry. Fights and violence break-out at games, bars, and on the street, because those involved became angry and lost control.

With the diamond mentality, you are in control of any emotion. In the beginning, God gave us dominion (control) over ourselves and our environment. There is nothing in the Bible that states that God took that control from us. The problem is that we fail to exercise the control we have. We also let the enemy tell us that we have no control, which is a lie that many of us believe. In *Ephesians 4:31*, it is stated that you should get rid of all bitterness, rage, and anger, brawling and slander, along with every form of malice. *Proverbs 15:1*, states that a soft answer "turneth away wrath;" but grievous words stir up anger. Then we are warned in *Proverbs 22:24*, "Make no friends with those given to anger, and do not associate with hotheads."

Yet we ignore the great advice and make best friends with those easily angered, to our detriment.

In *Genesis 1:26*, God gave dominion to man over all things. Other scriptures also support this. We fail to exercise this power that we have, and we submit to defeat with the usual excuse that I hear so often. "That is how I am, I cannot change," or "I am only human." Then I have to remind the person that they weren't born like that. It was them that changed into who they are now. This applies to all of us. We allow our circumstances in life to change us into who we are. That is both good and bad. It is good when we consciously choose to change into someone good, kind, and caring despite the negative things that happened to us. It is bad when we consciously or unconsciously choose to change to someone bitter and evil due to the negative things that happened to us.

Some people use excuses to justify their actions. For example, some people admit that they have to be mean so that people would not be unfair to them. They are of the opinion that people take advantage of kind people. That is far from the truth. No one can take advantage of you because you are kind. They take advantage of you because you allow them to do so.

Fear

I am sure you have heard some of the many stories about people who were stricken with fear. For example, as a result of fear, the person could not move a limb. Fear caused a friend of mine to wet his pants. Fear has caused some people to get a heart attack. There are so many more stories about things happening to people who were fearful.

Courtney was thick and tall and always looked older than his age. The other students feared him, and no one would dare mess with Courtney because of his intimidating structure. However, Courtney was a lamb on the inside and never got into fights. Thankfully because no one dared pick a fight with him. It was his looks, not him, that intimidated people.

One day a lady drove into the schoolyard and parked her car near the playing field. There was a small poodle in the rear seat of the vehicle. The lady got out of the car and made her way to the main building forgetting the car's rear window down.

We were sitting under a tree just on the border of the playing field and not very far from the lady's car. The playing field's border was lined with trees which the students used for shade from the hot sun. Suddenly, we heard barking and saw the poodle's head peeping out the car window. Courtney shouted and teased the small dog. The dog responded with barking and snarling, and we all laughed. Courtney then took a few steps towards the car while still teasing the dog. Suddenly and without warning, the dog leaped through the car window; and, at top speed, with a growl as menacing as a lion's roar, headed straight for Courtney.

When Courtney realized what was happening, he screamed, "The dog is going to bite me" and with that, he made a U-turn and ran towards the building with the dog in hot pursuit. The commotion attracted the other students who stopped what they were doing to watch this huge guy running from a small poodle that was in hot pursuit of him.

The building closest to the playing field had no doors to the playing field side; but only windows. The lowest window was about six feet from the ground. It was a great spectacle to see such a huge fellow fearing such a small dog. What we saw next, we could not believe. With the poodle not giving up and gaining ground on Courtney, he arched his chest, threw back his head, and gave it his all. With a leap that would put Clark Kent to shame, Courtney made a giant leap and landed on the window sill. He was the talk of the school for weeks on end. Even the Physical Education Teacher tried to get him involved in jumping after that. Fear can cause you to do things unimaginable.

Fear can cause you to move out of danger, or it can cause you to freeze up, putting you in further danger. It's not a good thing for you to be at the mercy of fear. Rather, it is better that you are in a position to control fear. The diamond mentality puts you in control of your fear.

Advantages and Disadvantages of Emotions

Emotions are very good, and without them, life would be very dull. Whether you are male or female, you have emotions. They are of great importance but, if not controlled, can do us much harm. Our emotions were not given to us to control us; we are to control our emotions. People gravitate towards people who show control and keep far from those who lack control. I shared the preceding examples to show how our emotions can affect us. Love, anger, and fear, if not controlled, can cause us to put our lives and the lives of others in danger. On the other hand, if these or any other emotions are brought under control, then we can greatly benefit from them.

According to the *Oxford* dictionary, *an emotion is an instinctive or intuitive feeling as distinguished from reasoning or knowledge. 2. A strong feeling deriving from one's circumstances, mood, or relationships with others.*

We, as humans, are capable of reasoning as opposed to animals, fish, birds etc. And, therefore, should not allow ourselves to be driven by instinct. Emotions, however, are fundamental, especially when there is not enough time to think. For example, you looked around just in time to see a vehicle bearing down on you and only 10-feet away. Your emotions can have several responses, but in many cases, your emotions will automatically "kick-in" to cause you to jump out the path of the vehicle saving your life. This type of emotion is critical, as we do not always have enough time to think under these pressured circumstances.

Emotions are like giants and have their places in our lives. By that, I mean emotions are very big and powerful and can make us do things that we regret later after the emotion subsides. To maximize the benefits of these giants, which some people find so difficult to control to the point that they surrender to them, we need to manage them. Otherwise, they will control us, and the outcome would not be so good because we were created to be in charge of all our being, emotions included. Imagine someone got angry with you and raised their voice at you. Every person present will expect you to react similarly and raise your voice as well. Imagine how shock they would be when instead of raising your voice, you lowered your voice and responded with, "I understand why you would be angry, but a smile would go better with that color tie." That response immediately transformed a mountain into a molehill.

Emotions Are Alive

Emotions move us to actions; hence that is why I say they are alive. I am sure you have seen or heard the things that emotions caused people to do. I have seen emotions moved people to tears, and I am included in there. I have seen emotions being the vehicle for harsh words to be spoken and friendships broken. I have heard about emotions being a great factor in the loss of lives. I have seen emotions inspiring people to give gifts, hugs, and kisses. These tell me that emotions are powerful and alive and can move people to do things, either positive or negative. Therefore, if not controlled, we will be at the mercy of our emotions. That is not how it is supposed to be.

For some people, it is more difficult. Those powerful emotions move inside of the person, driving them to do good or bad. Emotions capitalize or take advantage of the moment. If it is something positive, emotions can cause you to give more than what is considered normal. On the other hand, if it is negative, then emotions can also take advantage of that and move you to do something worse than what the average person would do. Those persons who find it more difficult to control their emotions are more prone to excessive behavior, whether good or bad.

Internal Conversations

Everyone has internal conversations going on at some time every day. That can be very distracting sometimes, especially when those internal conversations were triggered by something that activated our emotions.

Whenever a stressful matter occurs, you can reduce stress on yourself by deciding on a course of action to be taken. The longer you are indecisive, the more stress you take on. Do not have any internal conversations where you are continually replaying the adverse scenario in your mind. Internal conversations can be a great source of stress and distractions for you.

What goes on in your mind affects you and you only. Stop the blaming, self-pity, and trying to figure out "why me?" Make the decision, carry out the action and wait for the results. You may say that is not easy. That is where controlling your emotions comes in. After making the decision, move on to the next task and don't waste time trying to anticipate what the outcome will be. Remember, internal conversations are easily triggered by your emotions and are one of the culprits that contribute significantly to worry and stress.

How to Control Your Emotions?

So how do we control our emotions? This is very important. I am sure you have heard statements from both women and men that this is the way they are. They cannot change. That, however, is a false statement coming from a lack of knowledge. We are born with an almost blank slate, and everything else is learned. Therefore, whatever is learned can be unlearned. You can train yourself to control your emotions; you just need to put in the effort and remain focused.

When you wanted a university degree or a recognized qualification in a particular skill, you studied hard and diligently applied yourself. You wanted a house and a car, and again you worked hard and saved. You showed discipline and control so that you could save and have enough for that car and house. To control your emotions, you just need to apply these same skills and keep at it. Do not give up, for you will see results quicker than you expected.

Here are five steps that will help you to be in control of your emotions when you diligently implement them in your daily life:

Step 1

Accept That Others Are Entitled to Their Opinions and Beliefs

Let's, for example, take a person who has difficulty in controlling their anger. Someone says something that they dislike or disagree with, and they get hot and angry. They want to fight and shout like Greg. The first step in learning to control your emotions is to use the first step to the diamond mentality, that is, acceptance. Accept that others are entitled to their opinions and beliefs. Accept that others have a right to agree or disagree with you. Accept that you have a right to reject others' views without trying to force them to agree with you or adopt your perspective. Accept that humans can be similar but yet so different, which can be confusing at times. Accept that your friends and family will disappoint you sometimes, they are not perfect, and neither are you. That is why sometimes we think we know a close friend or family member, and then suddenly they do or say something that is totally out of character. Then you say to yourself, *I thought I knew this person but obviously not.* Accepting is such a powerful tool, that when you think about it and employ it in your life, you will see a huge difference just by doing that alone.

Step 2

Be Positive

Next, change your attitude to a positive one. Start to look at things from a positive point of view. Adopt an "I can do it mentality." Start to focus on looking for the solutions rather than focusing on the problems. Develop a solutions mentality. Have an attitude of being helpful. If you see something that needs to be done, don't wait for someone to tell you to do it. Take the initiative and do it. If you see someone in need of help, take the initiative and ask them if you can help them. They may refuse your help but asking helps you to change your attitude. Also, it gives you an opportunity to practice step number one, acceptance. It is their right to refuse your help, so don't get offended, and your emotions will remain in control. Say something complimentary or motivational to them and leave them. An example could be, I wish you a great day, or may you have great success in what you are doing. It is also important to say these things with sincerity so that you are not misinterpreted.

Step 3

Listen Effectively

Learn to listen effectively and thoroughly. Many times, we become upset and emotional due to one or two words that trigger our emotions. Later, we learn that the person did not intend it the way we interpreted it. If we had only listened to all the person was saying, we could have avoided that headache. Many times, you are trying to explain something to a person, and they interrupt you by responding with their answer, assuming what you were going to say, and their response is far from what you were trying to say. It is said that you are given two ears and one mouth so that you can listen twice as much as you talk. However, many people do the opposite; they speak twice as much as they listen. Listening effectively helps you control your emotions as you will no longer be an easy target for words that trigger your emotions. When you practice listening, you tend to weed out possible misunderstandings.

Step 4

Think Before You Speak or Take Action

Practice thinking before talking and taking action. To think before you talk or take action after hearing something that you don't agree with takes control. The more you practice this, the better you will become at controlling your emotions. You will no longer be impulsive and have regret at the things that simply jump out of your mouth. You will no longer be putting your "feet in your mouth" and having to apologize for your words or your actions. When you practice thinking before you talk or take action, you are able to come up with an appropriate action that is not influenced by emotions but is more objective and conducive to the situation at hand.

Step 5

Count

When you feel a negative emotion surfacing for whatever reason, try counting to fifty in your mind. If necessary, close your eyes, take a deep breath and exhale slowly while counting. That can help calm you and put you back in control of your emotions. This would also increase your concentration. Repeat the above as many times as necessary to bring that negative emotion under control. Speak to yourself and admonish yourself each time you slip up and let your emotions control you. This helps to remind you of your goal, that is, to be in control of your emotions. Practice these steps over and over until you are in control of your emotions.

Learning to control your emotions is very important. It is the lack of control that prevents you from reasoning and not listening to good advice. If you are a very emotional person, you may find it very difficult; however, it is not impossible. When you are able to control your emotions, you are less prone to being agitated. Internal conversations and worry are significantly reduced, giving you greater peace of mind. You become more objective in your thinking and in generating solutions.

Some people deliberately try to upset others. This often happens in the workplace. When you can control your emotions, it is very difficult for anyone to upset you deliberately or otherwise. You would now have a strategy that is really excellent for worry-free living, with some additional benefits. When someone's objective is to frustrate you, and they fail, they become frustrated that you are not frustrated. You don't need to retaliate; you don't need to waste any money, time, nor brain cells trying to do them wrong. You just need to control your emotions and be worry-free. Your enemies will catch a "fit."

Remember, you must practice the above five steps so that you gain control over your emotions. Just reading this information and not putting it into practice in your life would not help you. The diamond mentality is a way of living each and every day, so you must practice it in your daily life in order to reap the great benefits it has to offer.

I must confess that I was still trying to be in full control of my emotions at the time of writing this book. I have successfully implemented the other five life-changing habits. However, I have made tremendous progress in this area by implementing the above steps, and many circumstances that triggered my emotions in the past no longer do so. As a child, I was raised not to let anyone take advantage of me or talk in a condescending manner to me. Those are the two things that sometimes still trigger my emotions. I would estimate that I am about 95 percent successful in controlling my emotions. With that measure of success, I am confident I will be fully in control of my emotions very soon and have those two triggers under my belt.

For those with similar problems in these areas, here are three additional steps that will help you control your emotions against people who try to take advantage of you or talk to you in a condescending manner. They have certainly helped me.

Step 1

Don't Take It Personally

It is not about you. Most people who do that to you also do it to other people. They usually have a need to put down others so that they would feel good about themselves.

Step 2

Expect and Ignore This Type of Behavior

Expect some people to behave this way. When it happens, it would have less of an impact on you. Your response will be more controlled and not impulsive. You can then easily ignore the person and their behavior and diffuse an otherwise volatile situation.

Step 3

Give Feedback (If Possible)

Giving feedback is helpful to some persons, especially those who are not aware of the impact of their actions. Be cautious, however, in doing this, as not everyone would welcome your feedback, especially those who deliberately target you.

Chapter 7
Positive Thinking

Believe in You

If you don't believe in yourself, then who can you believe in? Our belief systems, the way we see ourselves, impact on the type of mentality we have. Whether we see the positive in things or not at all is due to our mentality which is shaped by our experiences and upbringing. Some people go through life thinking that the way they are now is how they are supposed to be. They believe they cannot change, and as a result, they do nothing about their situation. They just surrender to the circumstances they find themselves in.

You are not a statistic of life. You were created with and for a purpose. You were also created with a very important gift; the gift of choice. This gift is so important that when anyone tries to take it from us, we rebel. Whether we are children or adults, we rebel when our choices are taken from us. When you believe in yourself, you are not afraid to make choices, and you are ready to learn from your errors.

You have a choice in who you are and what you become. Your circumstances should never dictate that for you. Who you are and who you become are governed by your thoughts and choices and not by other people. Of course, there are some people who go around thinking that they can make you or break you. That is far from the truth; it is you that allow them to make or break you. The only one apart from yourself that can make or break you is God.

You have the power to decide who you want to be. It is, therefore, vital that you recognize the power of positive thinking. When you acknowledge that you are how you think, you can change anything about yourself simply by changing your thoughts. This becomes much easier when you believe in yourself.

Some people believe that they will never amount to anything, and they do not, due to the way they think about themselves. You can change the way you think about yourself from a negative thinker to a positive thinker. Start believing in yourself, believe that you can bring those dreams into reality. Have confidence that if you dream it, then you can achieve it.

I remembered, as a teenager, when anyone told me that I couldn't get something done, I would always ask them if someone had done it already. When they said yes, I responded with, if someone has done it, then so can I. It didn't matter to me who had done it before. Whether their IQ was higher than mine or not was unimportant to me. If they had qualifications that I didn't have was of no importance. For me, at that time, it was simply a case of, if someone had done it, then I too can do it. A few years later, I added to that "…and if no one has ever done it, then I will be the first." It was this way of thinking that helped me to succeed. It wasn't IQ and it wasn't qualifications. It was believing in me, and all that the Creator created me to be.

There are many people in this world, and some you may know, who are very qualified and have high IQs, yet they are not successful. Some become negative and bitter due to their situation. Some would say they were dealt a bad hand in life. However, we know, that even in an actual card game, a player may be dealt a bad hand; because he is a positive thinker, he does not give up but tries to win with the lousy hand he was dealt. In many cases, he is able to turn the tables in his favor and win the game. You, too, can turn the tables in your favor by thinking positive and leaning on God.

We don't only see this in card games; but in other games. In the Olympics, a runner gets a bad start and is last out of the box, but because he is a positive thinker, he refuses to give up; he is able to turn things around in his favor and win the race or make the first three. That all happened because they believed that they could do it. They believed in themselves and were positive thinkers, which came from a positive attitude. So how can we become positive thinkers?

Positive Thinking

Have you ever paused from your busy schedule to look at the world and see how it works with its various systems and people? If you haven't, I will encourage you to take the time now and pause and look at how things are happening around you. Don't try to put your opinion on what you see; just look and observe. If you had paused for just a moment, one of the things that you may have noticed is that birds of a feather flock together. That has nothing to do with the color of a person's skin. What I am talking about are personalities. Sparrows flock with sparrows, and ravens flock with ravens, and so on. That is because they have similar habits and do things similarly. Not because their feathers are the same color. The same goes for people. People are automatically attracted to other people with similar personalities to theirs. They don't need to know the person. They just walk into a room, and there is that connection. It is as if something is in the air. Maybe the aura they give off can be sensed by others with similar auras attracting them and drawing them to the person or group of persons that are similar to them.

In a multi-cultural city like Toronto, it is very easy to see what I am talking about. In my previous workplace, it was interesting to watch how a new employee would just automatically connect to the various groups without meeting them before. The gossiper instantly picked out the gossip group without being told. The flirt was also able to pinpoint that group with accuracy, and those that were goal-oriented and more serious about their work and about progressing in the workplace easily found that group. Of course, some individuals fit into more than one category and would span various groups.

It is said in the Holy scriptures (Proverbs 23:7 KJV) that as a man thinketh, so is he. From this, we can conclude that you are defined by your thoughts. This is easy to see because you may be aware that your actions stem or originate from your thoughts. For example, you may lie in bed and think about improving yourself. As a result of those thoughts, you applied and enrolled at an institution to learn a skill or improve upon an existing one. On another occasion, you thought to yourself that you haven't heard from your friend Tracy for a long time. You picked up the phone and called her. These two examples and many more, all started with thoughts. What you occupy your mind with the most, is what you will do or try to do the most.

According to James Allen, author of the book, *As a Man Thinketh*, "In his own thought world, each man holds the key to every condition, good or bad, that enters into his life and that by working patiently and intelligently upon his thoughts, he may remake his life and transform his circumstances." You may not give much thought to your thoughts, but the time has come for you to do so. To have a diamond mentality, you must be aware of what is in you and how that influences your actions. Everything that you do is preceded by a thought, whether you are aware of it or not. You have the power to restructure your thoughts.

Someone once said, greater than the victory of a thousand battles is the one who conquers himself. To conquer yourself is very difficult and entails knowing yourself or getting to know yourself. This is the most difficult of all battles. I believe this is the main reason that gossipers gossip and focus on others instead of themselves. It is very difficult to subdue oneself. It is easier to pull down and hurt others. Changing your way of thinking is not easy, but you can do it if you focus on you. Who you are today, is a result of your experiences and pain. You begin the journey of change by looking at yourself (introspection) and making a conscious choice to change for the better.

Many people believe and say that how they are now is how they were born. That is not true. You were born with an almost blank slate. As you grew and developed, you embraced certain attitudes and habits, some good and some bad. I am sure that they were things about you that you didn't like, and you changed those habits. Similarly, if there is something you don't like about the way you think then you can change it. If you think sick thoughts, you will be sick. If you think negative thoughts, you will be negative. If you think positive thoughts, you will be positive. If you think happy and joyous thoughts, you will be happy and joyous. The list goes on and on. Many times, people have asked me what I am thinking about that caused me to smile so sweetly. I usually respond that it was just a good thought, and that would be the truth. Your thoughts influence your moods and can cause you to be depressed, joyous, angry, or some other emotion.

Let's say, for example, you were in a bad relationship in the past. You managed to get out of it, but sometimes you would remember those bad things that happened to you. Those negative thoughts would automatically cause you to feel depress and sad. You do not want to have these depressive feelings as they make you unproductive and sometimes sick. You need to take those negative, depressing thoughts and replace them with positive and joyous thoughts. Positive thinking definitely helps you to overcome past bad experiences.

A person may ask or say, "but I don't have any good thoughts from my past, what do I do?" My suggestion in such a case is not to dwell on what you don't have but dwell on what you have, and you have a future. Think about how you would like to see your future. You may want to be joyous, happy, and successful. Think and dream about these things and plan a course of action on how to get there. Let these plans for your future become your dominant thoughts, and step by step, put the things in place that would help you realize them. The positive thoughts would bring smiles of joy to your face. As you achieve your goals, it will boost your self-esteem and bring happiness and even more positive thoughts to your life.

Many times, I have asked people a question about what they can do to help themselves. They immediately responded and told me what they cannot do or what they do not have. I then told them that I didn't want to hear about what they cannot do but what they can do. I cannot do anything with what they do not have. It then becomes a challenge to get them to tell me about the things they can do.

In many cases, I have to take the lead and give examples to get them thinking. It appears that such individuals spend so much time thinking and looking at what they do not have that they lost sight of what they have. They couldn't easily remember the things they can do.

When you start to think positively, you will begin to focus on your assets. That is, what you have and what you can do. Thinking about what you have and what you can do to improve are positive thoughts. Thinking about what you do not have and what you cannot do are negative thoughts and will make your life seem more difficult than it really is. The reason for that was stated above. I will repeat it for reinforcement because it is very important. This is it: You can do something with what you have, but you cannot do anything with what you do not have.

Therefore, you can see the power of your thoughts. Inventions are first discovered in the mind. It was a thought about flying like a bird and soaring like an eagle that led to the invention of the airplane. It was a thought about traveling in a carriage not drawn by horses that led to the invention of the motor car. Just look around you, and you would see the many inventions in your home and outside your home. These were all started with a thought. Eleanor Roosevelt once said, "Great minds think about ideas, average minds think about events and small minds think about people." Again, I ask: Which category are you in?

If you are not already in the category of a positive thinker, I would like to encourage you to get into that category now. Being a positive thinker helps you to move the mountains you will encounter in your life. The job is half-way completed when you approach it with positive thoughts. The things that daunt other people would not even faze you a little when you are positive.

Rodney rushed ahead of me to get the second to last item in the box. I asked Rodney, "Why did you rush to pass me? There are many boxes containing the same item."

He replied, "When you use the last item, you have to throw the empty box into the recycle bin."

I looked at him in disbelief and said, "But the recycle is only two steps away."

He said, "I know, but it seems so difficult."

I am still to figure out what is difficult about throwing an empty box in a recycle that is literally located two steps away. Your thoughts can make simple things seem difficult. I threw the empty box into the recycle before Rodney could turn to leave.

To have the diamond mentality, you need to be a positive thinker. This is crucial to the diamond mentality.

Changing the way you think is in your control. You need to have a "can do" mentality. Some people give up their true identity so they can fit in with the crowd. A crowd mentality could erode your positive mentality; therefore, you have to stop trying to fit in for the sake of fitting in. Rodney used to be a positive guy, but he didn't want to be singled out and be picked on, so he tried to fit in with the gossipers and naysayers. It wasn't long before he was behaving just like them, and his positive attitude had disappeared. Quickly after, he was suffering from physical problems and regularly complained to me about his stress level.

That need not happen to you. You are a game-changer. If someone has done it before, then you can do it, and if no one has done it before, then you can be the first. Choose wisely, those you hang-out with, otherwise, they can influence you to go back to your negative way of thinking. It is said, misery likes company. Never be misery's companion. Never be the companion of a person who gets angry quickly. Never be the companion of a negative person and never be the companion of a gossiper.

Companions and the Bible

Who you associate with can add to your stress or help you to live a stress-free life. Therefore, choose your friends wisely, otherwise, they can become burdensome and stressful to you. The Bible advises on the type of companions you should associate with. In *Proverbs 13:20*, it is written, *He who walks with wise men will be wise, but the companion of fools will suffer harm.*

People can drain you and add to your stress level. Therefore, it is very important to associate with those who are encouraging and positive; those who would check in with you to remind you to go after your dreams and stay far from those who would discourage you.

Proverbs 27:17 reads, *As iron sharpens iron, so one person sharpens another.*

This also shows you the importance of associating with like-minded persons. Those who would encourage you, add to you, and help you. In *Proverbs 22:24*, Do not make friends with a hot-tempered person, do not associate with one easily angered. This advice is golden and is worth so much if we will take it into our lives. I have seen friends trying to kill each other because of a hot temperament. I have seen friends pulling down each other as soon as their backs are turned. All of these situations lead to stress. If you desire a stress-free life, you need to choose your friends wisely and remove from you those that will add to your stress. Seek out positive thinkers as they will help you to be a positive thinker.

The Power of Your Thoughts

Everything we do starts with a thought, whether we are aware of it or not. Sometimes we messed-up because we didn't think through the process thoroughly. Someone would then say to us that we were not thinking; is that really so? We had to think of it to do it. The problem arose because we didn't think it through properly. Thoroughly thinking through the process increases your chances for success.

When something negative happens in our lives, our emotions are triggered, and our minds automatically take over. All manner of thoughts are injected into our mind and then spewed out; most of the time uncontrollably. These uncontrolled thoughts are what clog-up our mind like a sewage drain, and we have difficulty arriving at an accurate solution. By focusing on positive thoughts and possible solutions and not replaying the situation over and over in our minds we are actively seeking to resolve the problem and not worry.

For example, one morning I was a few steps behind a lady, as we approached the building of our work place. A person ahead of us saw us coming and held the door opened. The lady who reached the door first entered and held the door open until the person ahead of me reached the door. The first person then continued into the building once the next person had the door. The lady ahead of me, who was now holding the door, looked at me. I was about three steps away. She let the door close before I could reach it and walked away into the building.

The door automatically locked when closed, and could only open by fingerprint scan. I was new, and didn't have my fingerprint input into the system, so I depended on someone to open the door for me. I was at the door still waiting to enter when the same lady passed back by the door, looked me in the face, saw me knocking, and refused to open the door. A gentleman walking behind her saw me at the door and came and opened the door.

Most people would have been angry, would have confronted her, and told her off. I saw this as an opportunity to practice the diamond mentality. I first accepted I had no control over her actions. I maintained a positive attitude towards the whole situation. I made sure that I controlled my emotions so I won't get angry, and then I thought of her in a positive way. That quickly brought me to the position to go to her and tell her, "I forgive you for what you did. I do not hold anything against you. If ever you need someone to talk to, I am here to listen."

I was able to see this negative situation as an opportunity to practice what I had learn and I improved as a result. I responded with good to a person who just did me wrong. I let the lady know that she was forgiven and that I held nothing against her. Worry and stress were immediately eliminated and never stood a chance with a response like that.

To achieve the diamond mentality, you need to practice what you have learned. You can change the way you currently do things, to this stress-free way. People will continue to do you wrong and get on your nerve, that will never change, and you can never change that. That is a part of life. You can, however, do something about you; how you respond to negative people. Maybe your response to them can cause them to change.

Negative situations will continue to happen, that I am sure about. To conquer these situations, you must see these negatives as opportunities. Opportunities to practice the diamond mentality. Joseph Sugarman said, "The greatest success stories were created by people who recognized a problem and turned it into an opportunity." Every opportunity gives you the chance to build and equip yourself with these tools that you need, to have a stress-free life.

You, too, can train your thoughts to default to positive thoughts by filling your mind each and every day with things that are lovely, true, honest, just, and good. Keep away from gossip, slander, and un-forgivingness as these can pollute and burden your mind resulting in an increase of stress. Filtering what comes into your mind will result in a massive reduction of stress in your life.

As previously mentioned, your thoughts affect your actions. When a person does or says something negative to you, you must respond with positive thoughts and actions. Interestingly, responding with positive actions is easier than responding with positive thoughts. You may be aware that many people, maybe even yourself, respond with "positive actions" even when they don't really mean them.

For example, an unruly customer is giving a customer service representative an unnecessarily hard time. The rep responds according to his training and the rules of the company with actions that are considered positive by other customers and co-workers.

However, inside his mind, he wants to tell-off that unruly customer. That is what I am talking about. A person can behave in a manner that is not aligned with their mentality. However, thoughts are more difficult to control, and that rep. may be so disturbed by the events, that well into the next day, he may be having internal conversations about yesterday's situation.

With the diamond mentality, your thoughts must be positive and genuine. When you are able to do this, your actions are clearly seen as genuine. After an altercation with someone, you will no longer be having negative thoughts in your mind, mulling over and over for the whole day or even the entire week. That can be very stressful for you. Having genuine thoughts and actions would result in increased joy and happiness flowing from you and affecting all those present positively. When you go home after work, you will no longer feel drained and washed-out. You would have lots of energy for your family or get out-doors and enjoy other extra-curricular activities.

Eight Steps to Positive Thinking

Changing the way you think can be very challenging. It is not impossible but requires effort. Many people change the way their think after a painful event. Pain is a good motivator, but it is not necessary. The same way you can change after experiencing pain; the same way you can change before you experience pain. Changing now can prevent you from experiencing the pain and save you lots of disappointments and stress in the future. To shift your thoughts, to default to positive thoughts, you need to practice these eight steps daily:

Step 1
Fill Your Mind with Positive and Motivational Words and Quotes

Read lots of motivational material and quotes daily. Some people may already be doing this and can skip this step or even enhance it more. For those who find it difficult to find something nice to say, this is a very important step for you. You can only pull-out something from inside of you if it is already there. Fortunately for us, we can put anything that we desire inside us to help make us better people. In fact, you are in control of what goes in and out of you. Because you were exposed to something negative doesn't mean you have to let it reside in you. You have the power to kick it out. Don't just store this positive information that you receive but immediately share it with others. This will help to change your default to a positive one.

Step 2

Focus on the Positives in People and Life

When you practice focusing on the positives, it becomes easier to see the opportunities in all situations. After achieving this, your responses will automatically become more positive in undesirable circumstances.

Step 3

Definitely Give Up Gossiping, Refrain from Thinking and Speaking Ill of Anyone

I recently told a Christian lady that she should not get involved in gossiping. She responded, "If you don't gossip a little, then you won't have anything to talk about."

That is very far from the truth and an excuse to continue gossiping. They could discuss how to help the poor, homeless and elderly in the neighborhood.

You can find many positive topics to discuss and take action on. You can even take a negative matter and discuss the positives in it or discuss how you would like to see positive changes take place, making some positive suggestions.

Most importantly, the Holy Bible states in *Proverbs 20:19 (NRSV), A gossip reveals secrets; therefore, do not associate with a babbler.*

There are many more warnings in the Bible about gossip.

Step 4

Start Your Day with a Bold Assertion to Yourself

Every day, tell yourself in no uncertain terms that you will not allow anything or anyone to stop you from thinking positive and being positive.

Step 5

Be Grateful

Whether a thing is big or small, be grateful. Sometimes, we tend to appreciate only the big things in life and forget about the little things. Being grateful helps us to be more positive. Therefore, be grateful for everything, and you will be able to maintain a more positive mindset for a longer time.

Step 6

Keep Company with Positive Friends Only and Get Rid of All Your Negative Friends

This is a big one. We connect with people for various reasons. You will become like those you hang-out with. The Bible states in *1 Corinthians 15:33 (NIV), Do not be misled. Bad company corrupts good character.*

In *Proverbs 13:20*, it is stated, *Walk with the wise and become wise, for a companion of fools suffers harm.* It is very important to choose your friends wisely.

As a boy, my grandmother told me, "If you hang out with dogs, you will eventually eat dog food." Meaning, whatever your friends usually do, you will eventually do also.

Step 7

Ignore People and Things Whose Purpose Is to Distract

Sometimes, we respond to people and things that are there for the sole purpose of distracting us. These people and things are merely distractions. They affect our emotions, and we react. Hence, the importance of emotional control. Giving your important time to people and things that are there to distract you from your development or from making a meaningful contribution to those that need it, can add unnecessary stress to your life. It is important to know when to ignore and when to engage.

Step 8

Forgive Everyone That Has Done You Wrong

This single act cures you of hateful thoughts towards others, and it is you that benefit tremendously from it. Unforgiving does not affect the target person; it affects you and impacts negatively on your health.

As you can see, your thoughts are extremely important and dictate your every action. Therefore, it is imperative to train your thoughts to default to positive thoughts. When you achieve this, you will surely be closer to becoming a diamond.

Chapter 8
The Tongue — Control It

Functions of the Tongue

According to *webmd.com, the tongue is a muscular organ anchored to the mouth by webs of tough tissues and mucosa and at the back by the hyoid bone.*

The tongue is a mighty organ. You may know some or all of the things it is used for; but do you know how powerful it is? Given the problems that many people caused themselves and others due to the misuse of their tongue, I would say not everyone really knows the power of their tongue. The tongue has some very important functions; however, your tongue can be your worst enemy. It can be a great source of stress when used improperly.

As you know, the tongue is significantly used in the eating and drinking process. Because of your tongue, you can enjoy and experience the variety of taste and flavors in what you eat and drink. The tongue is also used for licking, and in many parts of the world, it plays a primary role in kissing and love-making, being used to transmit pleasures to one's partner. According to an article on tongue diseases on *www.pyroenergen.com*, your tongue can reveal early signs of disease.

The tongue is also used for speaking, and this is where the greatest amount of stress caused by this organ takes place. Many people carelessly say things that can cause problems in the lives of others and their own lives as well. The tongue is easily triggered by our emotions and when this happens, we blurt out things that we live to regret later. Therefore, being able to control your tongue is very important to your well-being and the wellbeing of others.

The tongue is used extensively in deception. When a person decides to deceive, he uses his tongue to carry out most of his plans. Unfortunately, when the perpetrator is exposed, which is usually the case, they end up with lots of stress as a result. It is also interesting to note that one of the things that the accusers will say is, "You said." This clearly shows that the perpetrator used their tongue in carrying out the deception.

The tongue is a source of life. In *Proverbs 15:4*, it is stated, "The soothing tongue is a tree of life." When the tongue is used in a positive way, it can be a very helpful tool. The positive and encouraging words you say to someone, even a stranger, can give that person hope. Your positive words can stop a person from committing suicide or from carrying out some heinous crime. Your positive words give life to others, to situations, and yourself.

The tongue is essential to our lives, and without it, we would have problems eating, drinking, and speaking. Just imagine not being able to taste your favorite food or drink, or even worse, have challenges swallowing them. Just imagine not being able to tell your loved ones how much you care about them and not being able to tell them you love them. Communication by the spoken word would definitely be a problem.

The Bible and the Tongue

In *James 3:8*, it is written, *but no human being can tame the tongue. It is a restless evil, full of deadly poison.* Unfortunately, that deadly poison affects us and sometimes ruins our lives. The Holy Bible speaks about the tongue very candidly and does not hold anything back when it comes to the tongue. In *Proverbs 18:21*, we read that the tongue has the power of life and death, and those who love it will eat its fruit. This is true as we can relate to the things that people have said that brought life to hopeless situations and death to lively situations.

For example, a person is on the verge of committing suicide because they believe that everyone is against them. Then, a simple statement like *I love you,* or *we care about what happens to you* can cause that person to change their mind from deadly thoughts to thoughts of life as they now believe that someone cares about them.

The opposite is also true when we speak death into situations that caused marriages to die, dreams to perish, hope to fade, and partnerships to become deceased. All because of someone allowing their tongue the freedom to spit out its venom.

"You cannot do anything right," says Herman to his wife, Betty. "You cannot clean, you leave the house dirty, and you don't take good care of the kids." That marriage soon came to an end as Betty couldn't go on taking the verbal abuse.

Kathy said to her law firm partner John, "I am sick of you and your laziness; I am the one carrying this firm on my back, and you just sit there and reap the benefits. You are a good for nothing son of a b…" It wasn't long after, that the partnership came to an end and could not be resurrected. Do you see the accuracy of the Bible?

When I was a young boy in primary school, I had a friend named Elvin, who went to the same school. His parents would always say to him, "you are mad, you are a trouble maker." By the time he reached eighteen, he was doing drugs and had encounters with the law. He was always getting into trouble. His own parents had spoken these things into his life from the time he was a child, and that was the life he had. Always be sure to speak positive things into the lives of your children.

In *1 Peter 3:10 (NIV)* it reads, *Whoever would love life and see good days must keep their tongue from evil and their lips from deceitful speech.*

So, if you love or desire a good life and want good days, you must control your tongue. This particular scripture gives you one of the tools for the diamond mentality. It says you must, not you may. You must keep your tongue from evil and deceitful speech. How can you do that? You must control your tongue. The tongue is a restless evil, full of deadly poison, but you can control it if you follow the steps to control your tongue. You need to be constantly vigilant, for the moment you let your guard down, your tongue will unleash poisonous words that is deadlier than the venom of a snake.

When a snake bites you, and you get medical attention quickly enough, your life may be saved. However, when careless words are spoken with or without thought of the consequences, there is no remedy, there is no antidote to heal those wounds, and they can eat away at you for years and years until you finally die. *Proverbs 15:4* reinforces it all when it states that, *the soothing tongue is a tree of life, but a perverse tongue crushes the spirit.*

All this is food for thought, and you should ponder on it.

It is said that the tongue cannot be tamed. That is true, but it can be controlled. The scripture says that a controlled tongue *is a tree of life (Prov. 15:4)*; *a well of life (Prov. 10:11)*; *a honeycomb (Prov. 16:24)*; *choice silver (Prov. 10:20)* and *good nourishment (Prov. 10:21).*

Control your tongue, and it will be well with you and others. Stay away from gossip and give a soft answer to turn away anger. Give healthy and helpful advice and guidance to those that ask. Be kind to your fellow man and tell him in a good way when he is wrong. That way, he may learn from the errors of his ways and stay away from gossip and tale-bearing.

Again, control your tongue. Sometimes our tongue can be our worst enemy. It is this small instrument that starts wars, breaks up relationships, causes you to lose out on excellent prospects, and adds fuel to countless situations. In the midst of a crisis, speak only if you have to and even then, make it very short. What you say at the time can escalate the problem. Therefore, do not react to the situation but give yourself time to assess the situation and the damage caused. Listen attentively, making sure your emotions are under control. Be focused and follow all the other steps at the end of this chapter before you speak. When words leave your mouth, they can never be taken back. Bite down on your lips to keep the words inside if you are having problems keeping your mouth shut. Words not spoken cannot cause any harm.

The Destruction of an Untamed Tongue

I had a manager who couldn't get along with most of his subordinates. At a heated meeting, which was usually the case, the inspectors asked for the union representative (rep.) to be present. The rep. came as requested, but the boss didn't think that he should be there. The boss hurled a barrage of insults at the rep. who was also a worker, demanding that he leave the room or else he would throw him out.

I was not prepared for what happened next. The boss got up from his seat, went over to the rep. and physically tried to throw this big burly guy out of the room. The boss is about half the size of the rep. A scuffle ensued, and in less than thirty seconds, the boss was knocked unconscious. If only he had held his tongue, spoken kind words, and respected the workers' rights. That life-threatening situation and the worrying and stress that followed would have been avoided.

The tongue can cause untold worries in your life. Excessive worrying causes stress that produces harmful hormones in your body and breaks down your immune system, finally making you sick. Some types of sickness can kill you. It is easy to conclude that worrying can kill. Why then would you want to keep it or embrace it? I say embrace because the way some people talk about worry, it is as if it was a friend, a buddy that you don't want to lose. These people make worrying sound like a good thing.

In the same breath, they complain as if they didn't want it. The confusing signals they send you. When you try to help, they are always quick to tell you what wouldn't work. Nothing would work as far as they are concerned. They love to worry so much, they won't even try one of the suggestions you mentioned that would cost them nothing; all because they do not wish to be parted from their dearly beloved "worry." These types of people are the worry lovers.

Debra, one of my past workmates, would say to me with a big smile on her face, "I am always worrying, I can't help it, I must worry. If I don't worry, then something is wrong with me."

I would tell her that worry will make her sick if she doesn't control it. Some years later, Debra was diagnosed with a tumor in the brain. Her life was changed forever. Her words also changed, but that was a bit too late. Do you want that to happen to you? I certainly would not like that for you. Don't wait until it's too late to change.

So how can you control your tongue and prevent unnecessary worries from invading your life and the lives of your loved ones and friends? Here is how. Remember that to achieve anything good and worthwhile, you must put in the effort. You must make an effort. You will not regret having taken back control of your life from the enemy. The enemy is so skillful that he makes us think we are in control when, in truth, we are not.

As long as you believe or feel that you are in control, you will never do anything about your situation. If you truly believe that you are in control, then ask yourself and honestly answer yourself: Why do you say things and then regret that you said what you said? Don't make any excuses for the slip-up. It is simple; you slipped-up because you were not in control. You thought you were, but you were not.

I confess that this is an area that I am still working on. It is incredibly challenging because it is tied to your emotions. I have, however, made significant progress, and so can you. Follow the steps below daily and the various tips found in this chapter, and you will soon have control over your tongue. Remember the diamond mentality is a way of life; that means you have to live it each and every day.

Floyd was being his usual self—saying things without thinking about the consequences when Brenda passed by. Floyd said to Brenda, "I was just talking to your best friend, and she said you need to lose weight."

Brenda immediately became infuriated. Without asking a question, she stormed into the office and unleashed a verbal attack on Tasha; telling her that if she would mind her business, she would still have her husband.

That was the end of a good friendship between Brenda and Tasha all because of the careless use of that powerful instrument in Floyd's mouth called the tongue. Of course, there are other factors that came into play that contributed to the destruction of this relationship. Many of us can relate to this or similar stories that caused lives to be wrecked because of the lack of control of the tongue.

One of the most under-mentioned parts of our body yet one of the most powerful is our tongue. You very seldom hear a conversation about the tongue. Yet, it is the very thing we use to have conversations. In fact, we cannot have a conversation without the tongue. Yes, we can communicate without the tongue but conversation, no. In the above scenario, it was the tongue that brought death to that relationship. One of the deadly effects of the tongue is death.

There are many conversations about the eyes, the ears, the lips, even the neck but seldom the tongue. Maybe because it is hidden, and we rarely see it unless a person sticks it out. A few people like to do that, even popular singers. Perhaps it is because it is heavily used for eating and everything associated with eating. Whatever the reason the tongue is underrated and this needs to be change so that people come to realized what a powerful instrument they are walking around with. Maybe then they will make an effort to keep it under control and prevent it from spewing the venom that destroys the lives of others.

The Tongue and the Diamond Mentality

We use the tongue to say so many things. Some of those things can make a person feel good, and some can really hurt or damage a person. I received a phone call from a friend of mine one evening. I realized she was crying, and asked her what was wrong. She replied that her husband had just told her some hurtful things and called her insulting names.

She had confronted him about an affair she knew he was having, and he retaliated by telling her very hurtful and insulting things as if she was at fault. I could hear in her voice that she was really broken. I was at a loss for words initially, but after saying a quick, silent prayer for words of wisdom, the words came to me. I told her that she was wonderfully and beautifully made; so don't accept what her husband told her.

I then reminded her of her accomplishments in life and that she was actually living her dream. I told her to focus on those things, and she would see that all that her husband had said were all lies. She pondered for a moment and agreed. I also told her to forgive him as not forgiving will do her more harm than him. Again, she agreed. By the time she got off the phone, her spirits were mended, and she was feeling good again. The tongue had restored life and hope to this broken woman. A tamed tongue is advantageous to others and yourself. You will be speaking life into situations, into the lives of others, and into your own life.

So, you see, the tongue is very powerful; in fact, I will say it is very, very powerful. It can make a person feel really good and motivate them to positive actions, and it can hurt, destroy and cut like a two-edged sword. It can even drive a person to suicide. Sadly, many people find it difficult to control their tongue. They just opened their mouth, and the tongue goes to work. However, I have good news for you. You can control your tongue. You can choose to use your tongue to make a positive difference in the lives of others. It just requires some effort on your part. Below are eight suggestions to help you control your tongue.

8 Steps to Controlling Your Tongue

Step 1

Take a Deep Breath and Hold It

When you are told something that can cause you to get emotional and react by saying something that you may regret later, take a deep breath through your mouth, hold it and count to fifty (50). If you are still angry and out of control after that, then repeat it. This actually buys you time to cool down and get in control. You can't speak and breathe in through your mouth at the same time. Also, you cannot hold a deep breath and speak effectively.

Step 2

Control Your Emotions

A slip of the tongue tends to happen most often as a result of uncontrolled emotions. If you haven't done so yet, you will need to go back to *chapter 6* to learn how to control your emotions. As stated in that chapter, emotions are good but if you are not in control, they can wreak havoc in your life and the lives of others. It is very important not to react prematurely and to remain calm. Being able to control your emotions puts you in the driver's seat.

Step 3

Listen Effectively

Sometimes a person may not clearly or accurately communicate their intentions. You may receive the wrong message unintentionally. This could trigger your emotions resulting in the unleashing of your tongue. That has certainly happened to me. It is, therefore, vital to listen effectively and fight that urge to react prematurely. It's not always about you; the person may just be having a bad day and dumping some of their garbage, unfortunately, on you. So, when you have finished listening, say something positive or motivational.

Step 4

Accept Responsibility for Your Actions and Stop the Blame Game

One of the first things we say in reacting to people telling us that we should not have said what we said is to blame the other person. "She made me say it" or "He went too far, so I had to tell him off."

Stop blaming. You are responsible for your tongue and not your tongue responsible for you. It is you that have to take charge of what comes out of your mouth. Be responsible for your actions, and your words, and this will help you control your tongue. You will now be aware that it is your fault, not the other person's. It is you that have to bear the consequences for what comes out of your mouth.

Step 5

Think Before You Talk

Process the information that you just received before opening your mouth. You don't need to respond immediately to everything. Ask for some time out or tell the person that you need time to think about what they just said, and you will get back to them soon.

This works like a miracle, and it has two outcomes. First, it does what I just told you. It gives you time to process the information so that you can have a much better and control response, and secondly, it gives you time to cool-down.

What the person had said to you could be very hurtful and distasteful. You immediately felt like retaliating with some harsh words that you may have regret later. Taking time out causes you to cool-off so that you can clearly think and have a much better response. You may later realize that the person said what they said because they were misinformed or were simply having a terrible day. For example, a person can become frustrated or angry after receiving news that their father was diagnosed with cancer and didn't have long to live.

When you learn to control your tongue, a whole new avenue will be opened up to you. You will become aware that people do things for reasons unknown to you and unknown to themselves. People lash-out at others for a variety of reasons. Simply having a bad day can cause a person to say hurtful things. Without the diamond mentality, you are unaware of how to overcome these problems in life and respond like the beautiful diamond you are. So, the next time a person says something unpleasant to you. Let them know they can tell you what is bothering them, and you can be a friend to them and help them through their difficulty.

Step 6

Forgive

After you have thought about what the person said to you, you may still be angry, or become angrier. This is very possible because you may become aware that this was really an unwarranted attack on you; this was personal and had nothing to do with the person having a bad day or a crisis in their life. So, this can and most likely will make you very angry.

Not forgiving can build resentment in you. This resentment will result in you having a low tolerance for that person or any person perceived to be similar. That means that the slightest thing that person says to you can make you angry and cause you to say something you may regret.

This would make it more difficult for you to control your emotions but not impossible to do so. Take a few deep breaths to help you control your anger and you must choose to forgive them. Yes, I say "must" because forgiveness is really about you and not so much the other person. Unforgivingness can cause untold problems in your life because you are carrying around a problem in your mind that is nagging at you. This can ruin your health, destabilize your family, and cause your career to crumble before your very eyes.

Notice that these things are happening to you, not the other person. They are happening to you because of the unforgivingness. Something that many people don't realize is this. When you hold a grudge against someone, that person does not know what is in your mind so it is not bothering them. When you have unkind or evil thoughts towards someone, that person does not know about those thoughts, and hence they are not affected. It is your life that is going down the drain as a result, not theirs.

Note that if it is a situation that you need to respond to immediately. For example, a work situation where your boss said something to you that was hurtful, and you think you need to respond immediately. Take a deep breath or several deep breaths and try to bring your emotions under control quickly before speaking. A moment of silence for this process to take place is quite fine. So do not worry about the silence. It is more important to have a positive response as an erratic and negative one can cause you to lose your job or get demoted.

Step 7

Stay Away from All Forms of Gossip, Slander and Tale-Bearing

What your tongue is customary to spewing out, it will spew out automatically. Listening to gossip is just as bad as talking about it. You are actually providing an outlet for gossip to continue to circulate. Therefore, do not even listen to gossip, or it will take you over again. Not listening to gossip and slander will also prevent your tongue from getting involved.

Step 8

Develop the Habit of Speaking Positive Things

Regardless of who we are, we sometimes slip up and respond to a situation without much thought. What happens in such a case is that we automatically switch to our default. That is, we will say the things that usually come out of our mouths without effort. Therefore, if you are accustomed to saying positive things, then positive things will automatically come out of your mouth. If you are accustomed to speaking negatively, then negative things will automatically exit your mouth. It is, therefore, important to create habits of doing the right things. So, create a habit of speaking positively by doing so at every opportunity. Positive words can defuse an explosive situation.

Remember that just like a stone that is thrown from your hands, so are the words of your mouth. Once they are released from your mouth, they cannot be stopped or taken back. The damage is done. "If I had known" always come too late.

Once you have mastered these eight steps, you will be able to control your tongue. You will have more control over your situations and less stress in your life. You will be a healer rather than a destroyer.

This is also the last of the six life-aligning principles. When you master all six, you will conquer stress and stress-related illness. You would be more productive in all areas of your life while having more energy for your family and doing the things you love. You will be a beautiful diamond.

Chapter 9
The Diamond Mentality
at Home and Work

Relationship with Your Family

With the diamond mentality, you have nothing to lose and everything to gain. Your health is the most important thing that you have after your life. Although your health is second only to your life, it influences your life tremendously. Your health plays a vital role in every area of your life. The diamond mentality will positively affect your health, giving you the opportunity to enjoy life to the fullest.

The diamond mentality is beneficial to you in every area of your life: At home, work, recreation, traffic jams, mishaps, problems, and in all other areas. The beauty of the diamond mentality is that you do not react to stressful situations like other people; you respond.

When I was in my 20s, I would hang out with some "friends" on weekends. This was mainly a male group although from time to time there were females. Most of us were single except for two, David and Percy. We were working young men with varied professions, from construction workers to lawyers.

Percy was married and would often complain about his wife. He hated going home, so he will beg us not to end the evening session too early. We would usually meet after work on Fridays, around 5:30 pm. Some would arrive as late as 7:00 pm, depending on how their workday ended.

Percy will do everything to get us to stay at the bar for long periods. The bar would usually close at midnight on Fridays. 11 pm would come and go, and Percy wouldn't want to go home. The reason was that Percy wanted to go home at a time that, according to him, his wife would be sleeping, and he can slip into bed without her asking him any questions because the slightest thing, and they were quarreling and fighting. He just couldn't handle the situation at home, and his strategy was to stay away as long as he could.

Percy's life at home was stressful. He had nothing good to say about his wife. It made you wonder why he married her in the first place. He would work late hours during the week or find another bar to go to if he wasn't working late. Home for Percy became just a place to sleep and shower. I am sure you may know people like that who are stressed by their home environment to the extent that they avoid going home. They make excuses to go by mum, visit their siblings, or hang out with friends.

David, on the other hand, had a different situation in his marriage. He would sometimes invite his wife to hang out with the group. She knew exactly who he was hanging out with. David had a set time to be home with his wife, and without fail, every Friday night, he would simply tell the guys it was time for him to go home to his wife. He didn't make any excuses; he simply said it like it was. Of course, some of the guys tried to pressure him to stay longer by telling him he was the boy and his wife was in control. Therefore, he had to go home, otherwise his wife will put him in the dog house. David never tried to argue. He will simply say, "This 'boy' is going home to his wife," and with that, he departed.

At that stage of my life, I didn't know God, and I knew nothing about the diamond mentality. David was better at handling situations, and in my opinion, he handled his situation very well. In fact, when I got married, I borrowed a few ideas from him, which were very helpful.

With the diamond mentality, you will be equipped for every stressful situation in your family. In fact, the principles of the diamond mentality are so diverse that they not only help you to handle and manage stressful situations, they also help you to build positive relationships in all areas of your life, even with the in-laws.

When your spouse raises his/her voice at you, and you respond with something like, "You're so much lovelier when you speak calmly." That type of response will diffuse the tension in the room giving the opportunity for both of you to make amends. As you know, when both of you try to out-do each other by raising your voices, it only causes the problems to escalate.

With the diamond mentality, you no longer have to make excuses to be away from home. Why? Because you can now manage with grace any negative situations at home. You will be equipped to handle stressful situations and resolve conflicts with the ones you love and among the ones you love without stressing yourself. Your home will have peace and will truly be your castle. You will love being at home spending time with your loved ones.

Children can be a major source of stress if they are not obedient. If they are bent on getting into trouble, your life can be misery. Lana was a friend of mine. Her daughter, Priscilla, at age 14, was very strong-willed and chose to do the things that were harmful to her. Of course, Priscilla didn't think so. She was of the opinion that her mother was too strict and didn't want her to enjoy life. This caused her mother many sleepless nights as they would argue and fight over Priscilla's bad choices.

Priscilla ran away from home several times. On one of those occasions, she had moved in with a man nearly three times her age. The police were involved as she was under-aged. Her mother was so stressed she could not sleep well, and her face was covered with pimples due to the stress from Priscilla's behavior. Unfortunately, I didn't have the knowledge of the diamond mentality at that time. All I could do was listen and empathize.

You may know of someone like that who is going through problems with one or more of their children. This book doesn't give you solutions to these problems, but it shows you how to handle these problems in such a way that your stress level as a result of these problems is greatly reduced. The techniques given will help you to be in control of your emotions and fears. They will help you make good choices and show love and empathy to your family and fellow human beings. The diamond mentality can contribute to resolving the issues with your children. There will always be problems in life. The diamond mentality helps you handle and resolve those problems in a manner that is not stressful and good for your health.

Every type of problem found in the home can produce some amount of stress. These stress levels are greatly reduced when you have the diamond mentality. When these six principles are incorporated into your life, on a daily basis, you and your family will benefit greatly. You and your family will have the happy life you all deserve free from stress and stress-related illness. You will also have more energy at the end of each day for your family because stress drains your energy. Therefore, the lack of stress will definitely energize you. I have experienced this over and over, and it is simply awesome.

The In-Laws

Your in-laws can get on your nerves sometimes. Some parents just don't know when to let go and can actually contribute to the destruction of the marriage. Cepheus was such a case. He related his story to me as to the major problem in his marriage. He said that his father-in-law would call his daughter every morning around 5 am. When he didn't call, he would just show up at approximately 6 am. Cepheus could never spend quality time with his wife in the morning due to her father always calling or coming by early. He talked to his wife about it, but she made the world of excuses for her father. She didn't want to offend him. That pushed them so far apart that eventually, they separated and later divorced.

How Cepheus reacted to his father-in-law added fuel to the fire. That fire eventually burned their marriage to cinders. With the diamond mentality, you will not react to your in-laws. Instead, you will diligently respond to them with peace and love so that they may understand that love is about life. Life is in all things. To love your children is to want them to be happy and to have a marriage that is healthy and full of life. Therefore, their actions should help provide the necessary nutrients that would contribute to the life of the marriage and not drain the marriage of its life.

What are the benefits of having the diamond mentality at home? You will enjoy peace and tranquility in your home. No longer will you dread having to go home to that nagging wife or husband; because you will have the right response. You will be able to remain calm, cool, and composed. You will be a king or queen in your castle. Your relationships with your partner and your children will improve tremendously as you live the diamond life. Your in-laws will no longer cause chaos but harmony that will contribute to a lasting marriage. You will have a lot more energy for your family at the end of each day.

The Diamond Mentality at Work

The home and workplace are the two places that most people spend the majority of their time. Interestingly, enough these two places are the two highest sources of stress. Some people get most of their stress from the workplace; others get most of their stress from the home; and unfortunately, some get most of their stress from both.

Your workplace demands that you are productive while on their time. It is only fair that you are productive in your job as you are paid to produce. You are paid for your time.

Doing the opposite is plain dishonesty. When you have the Diamond Mentality, you will have less down-time. You will not get involved in gossip or be distracted by small non-essential things. You will maximize the use of your time in the workplace to get results.

Standing or sitting around complaining about a new rule in the workplace is very unproductive. Instead, use the suggestion box or a formal meeting to voice your concerns, and be sure to add recommendations. Just complaining is not good enough. Use the principles of the Diamond Mentality in the workplace by accepting the rules that govern the workplace, having a positive attitude and behavior, being positive, and controlling your emotions. Always look to see what you can change about yourself first before you ask another person to change. The problem just might be you.

When the boss gives you a task to complete with a very tight deadline, you will not waste time sharing with your workmates that your boss thinks you are a super-person. Instead, you would immediately work out a plan to get the job accurately and efficiently done within the given time. Too often, we waste the limited time we have worrying or fretting over a task given to us or over differences of opinions on how the task should be done. Once a decision has been made, jump on it, and you will see that the amount of time you save is phenomenal.

There is a belief in many workplaces that if you care about your work, you must get stressed to show that you care. I actually heard, one guy, who is part of the management team, stated in a meeting that getting a little stressed over your job shows that you care. My question would be, how much stress is safe, and how does a person measure that? Unfortunately, the floor was not open for questions.

Interestingly, this belief that being stressed shows that you care is perpetuated by management and comes all the way down the line. This is a lie that was devised a long time ago to keep workers in bondage; and continues. Today's managers and business owners are not aware of this lie, and so they believe it and actually feels good when a worker is stressed about a situation in the workplace. They too become stressed as well, because they believe that is the thing to do. Let me prove to you that it is a lie that if you stress on the job, then you care about the job.

First, let me repeat the lie: *If you care about your job then you must become stressed when issues arise to show that you care.*

Now let me show you why that is a lie, and hopefully, many people will stop it, hence we will have healthier work environments. It has been proven by scientists and doctors that stress leads to illness and sometimes death. We can safely say that stress kills. Now, if stress kills, and that has been proven, why would anyone want you to be stressed. Let us now revisit that statement and use the scientific conclusion that stress kills.

If you care about your job, then you must become ill or kill yourself (become stressed) when issues arise to show that you care. Now, does that make sense? Have I proven to you that what you have been doing to yourself is very unhealthy and does not equate to caring? Would someone that cares about you ask you to do something that can kill or harm you in any way? Two of my friends died at a young age on the job from complications arising from heart disease. According to *www.medicinenet.com*, stress can cause heart problems and high blood pressure.

Caring is about finding solutions quickly. It is about reducing wastage and trying to maximize profits. Caring is about respecting everyone in the workplace regardless of class creed or color. If your child became ill in your presence, would you become stressed and worry and run around complaining to everyone, or would you call an ambulance immediately? You see, calling the ambulance is a way of trying to get a solution for your loved one. Becoming stressed and complaining to others about why it shouldn't happen to your child amounts to doing nothing and will not help her situation but may cause her life.

After your company invests hundreds of thousands of dollars annually towards training staff, why would you want to kill them? Why do you want to kill yourself? Human resources are the most important assets of a company. It doesn't matter how many computers you have. It doesn't matter how much machinery you have. It doesn't matter how much technology you have. If you don't have healthy and competent staff, then your business is going nowhere. If your staff is regularly sick, then you are losing lots of money. If your staff is dying regularly and you have to train new staff regularly to replace them, you are losing lots of money.

Recently, a friend of mine, who is actually on the management team, had to be home on sick leave for three weeks for stress-related illness. She was overworked and stressed because top management was slow to replace a key position that was vacated for five months. As a result, she had to take up the slack, which involved her working long hours dealing with additional customer issues. Her stress level went through the roof, and her back and neck were seriously affected. There was now no one to do either job for three weeks.

Had management understood the negative impact their slow decision-making will have on that staff member and their business, they would not have done it. As soon as she was back to work, the company quickly filled the vacant position. Something terrible had to happen to a key person to get management to act quickly. Thousands of dollars would have been lost over those three weeks. All of those problems could have been avoided if they had known and understood that stress equals sickness and time off from work and could even mean death.

All companies, regardless of their product, will encounter challenges from time to time. Some companies, more frequently than others, due to the very nature of the product. What a company really wants is that when there is a problem or challenge, the staff members involved will be focused on getting a solution quickly and not being stressed over the situation. When a staff member becomes stressed over a situation, they are unable to focus on getting a solution or helping the team to come up with a solution.

Take Shalene, for example. Shalene has the type of personality that panics at the slightest thing that goes wrong. There was a problem with the product. Shalene was the one that spotted the problem, and she was also part of that team. She started her usual outburst, "Why is this happening? Oh God, I can't understand why these things are always happening to me."

She ran over to the workstation next to hers and repeated the same things to that team which had nothing to do with her product, thereby distracting them from their tasks. She then went halfway across the floor, moaning and complaining about her issues. Her teammate had to figure out a solution all on his own. Luckily, her teammate was solution-focused and by the time she returned after complaining and crying out to everyone, he had the problem solved. When asked why she didn't help to find a solution, she said she helped with the solution because she was worried. "You have to be worried when there is a problem," she said.

I saw a similar situation like that in a different work environment. I was an economist at that time. The minister called the supervisor, another worker, and myself to his office. He asked us to produce a report with research and statistics by the end of the day as the prime minister wanted it urgently for a meeting. After leaving the minister's office, the supervisor and the other worker engaged in conversation about how unfair and unrealistic the deadline was, given the depth of the work he wanted. I immediately excused myself from their conversation, went to my office, and started to do my portion. Before the end of the day, I had completed my part, and the other two were still struggling to get started.

Complaining never solves problems. Stressing yourself never solves problems, and most noteworthy, gossiping never solves problems. When your employees are equipped with the diamond mentality, they become more focused on the task at hand. They become solution-focused and not complaining-focused. Productivity increases because less time is used on gossiping and trivial matters. There is less time away from work due to illness because stressful situations are handled in such a way that workers are not stressed.

The diamond mentality is very beneficial in the workplace. Before your employees had the diamond mentality, they wasted days complaining about the decisions made just because there went against what they had suggested. Much time was also lost on sick leave. Problems took a longer time to be solved. After the diamond mentality was introduced to the workplace, productivity was positively impacted. Employees no longer brought to work their problems from at home and allowed them to affect their moods, energy, and productivity. They became solutions-focused and not problem-focused. They avoided gossip and trivial distractions in the workplace. They became more focused on the task at hand, and the company's profits were increased.

The Diamond Mentality in Clubs and Not-for-profit organizations

Many people spend an hour or two per week on extra-curricular activities. Some people spend more. If you are retired, you may spend a whole lot more time at your club. The active individual likes to be involved in doing many things, utilizing his/her time to benefit others and themselves. Involvement in multiple activities can result in a fast-paced life of moving from one activity to another. Whether it is travelling from work at the end of the day to the football club, or commuting from volunteering at the food bank to the weekly bingo night, situations will arise that can be stressful. It is, therefore, important to be able to manage these stressful situations in such a way that you are not stressed.

All clubs and not-for-profit organizations have one thing in common with the workplace, and that is people. You have to interact with people. As long as there are people interacting, then there will be friction and disagreements among members. How these challenges are handled would determine the level of stress you will encounter at your club and how much you enjoy your time at your club.

When you incorporate the diamond mentality into your life on a daily basis, you are actually equipping yourself with the tools to handle every diverse situation. The diamond mentality is very important to all persons in every type of organization. When individuals in an organization have the diamond mentality, there is more camaraderie, problem-solving, and focus on the business of the club or organization.

These principles can be applied to any and all organizations, whether it is a not-for-profit club, a sports team, a PTA, or an international organization like the UN. That's because, in all organizations, they are people, culture, resources, tasks, problems, and solutions. These are the things that cause people to argue, disagree, and needlessly worry; among other things. The good news is that you don't need to worry or be agitated. By applying these principles, you will have the diamond mentality regardless of the organization in which you are involved. I can safely say that the skills you acquire are transferable to all areas of your life; at home and outside the home.

I, too, have been a member of many clubs for most of my life, from karate to chess, theatre and toastmaster's clubs. I know that the main activity was not the only thing that moved me to attend meetings every week and, in some cases, multiple times per week. There is a joy that you get from interacting with people that have something in common with you. There is fun at the club meetings, and that motivates you to come back week after week. However, there are also contentions that can steal that joy and interrupt the beautiful interactions between members. The diamond mentality will give you the tools to prevent disagreements from escalating and maintain the joy between the members.

The Diamond Mentality on the road

Driving is one of the most stressful activities for some people. The slightest thing and some drivers will totally lose it. Road rage is quite common and shows that stress doesn't only cause you to be ill. It can also cause you to endanger the lives of others and change your life forever.

Imagine you are driving along and suddenly "wham!" a vehicle rear-ends you. How do you respond? Some drivers would jump out of their vehicle uncontrollably, filled with anger and wanting to beat the living daylights out of the driver that ran into the back of them. I have seen situations like that.

With the diamond mentality, you remain in control of the situation from beginning to end. Even if the other driver loses it, you are still in control. This control can greatly help diffuse potentially dangerous situations for you and your family, as violence can easily explode if fed and you will not be feeding it. The diamond mentality is the perfect solution to any and every situation that can result in a stressful situation.

I saw what I believe to be one of the least likely situations on the road that could result in an accident. Yet it caused one of the drivers to be so enraged, that there was almost a confrontation. Thanks to the other driver, who totally ignored the irate driver and kept driving, the situation was not further escalated.

One driver stopped at the red lights. I was immediately behind this driver. The lights turned green, and so the driver started off. A driver on the road to the right who was making a right turn, continued to turn ahead of the vehicle in front of me. There was more than enough room, in my opinion, for the turning driver to turn and be ahead of the vehicle in front of me. All went well, and the turning driver was safely ahead, without the driver going straight having to brake unnecessarily. To my surprise, the driver in front of me sped up and changed lanes. He drove next to the driver that had turned and started to shout at him. The driver then avoided the situation by moving into another lane as it was a four-lane road. The aggressive driver followed suit and continued shouting through his window while driving. Fortunately, there was an exit to a highway, and the driver took that exit. The aggressive driver couldn't follow as there was no room to cut across the lanes at such a short distance. That situation was unnecessary and could have been easily avoided if the aggressive driver had the diamond mentality.

Stress from driving can be considerable for some people. Accidents are not the only culprit. Traffic jams get the better of most people as they are not going anywhere and they need to be someplace. They are those that cut you off abruptly and have you braking suddenly, or worse, those that cut in front of you and then immediately slow down. Then there are the pedestrians that stroll lazily across the road without a care in the world or while using their cell phones totally oblivious to the oncoming traffic.

When you have the diamond mentality, you can respond to every road challenge in ways that do not stress you. If you are on your way to work and encounter a problem on the road, it does not negatively impact your entire day. You are able to arrive at work with calmness and ready to do a good day's work. This is the nature of the diamond mentality. You are happier overall, and most importantly, you, your family, and your workplace benefit tremendously.

Chapter 10

The Diamond Mentality and
Death, Sickness, and Finances

Death

Regardless of who you are and how good you are at managing adverse situations, there are a few events in life that overthrow just about everyone. These are: the death of a loved one, ill-health, and being financially broke. If you truly think about it, life is really a death sentence. That is, from the time you are born, there is a time appointed for you to die.

When you lose someone, who was very close to you to death, it can be devastating. Some people take months and even years to overcome grief. As a result, their health suffers and, in some cases, they quickly go to join the departed one. The death of a loved one usually takes a toll on those that are left behind.

Charles was a past workmate of mine who was an excellent conversationalist and very humorous. I thoroughly enjoyed talking to Charles regularly because of the varied subject matters that we would discuss. He was a man of ideas and was able to put over his ideas in an interesting way well weaved with humor.

Charles's mother died after a short bout of illness, and Charles took it very hard. You could see the difference in him as he tried to balance work while helping to make arrangements for his mother's funeral. You were allowed two weeks of special leave from work for the death of very close family members. However, Charles said he wanted to work as it helped him take his mind from his mother's death.

The funeral came and went. Three days after his mother's funeral, his father suddenly died. Charles had previously told me that his mother and father were very close, and her death was taking a toll on him. With his father's death coming so close on the heels of his mother, Charles was now further devastated. Even the way he walked was unsteady. Charles was never the same again. Two years later, and Charles still didn't feel like talking or laughing as he used to. When you looked at his face, he looked like he had aged by ten years in a matter of months.

The death of a loved one can change us. It can rob us of our joy and happiness if we allow it. Death can demotivate us and make us angry and bitter. That's why some people ask the question, "why did it have to happen to me?" It need not be so. This is one of the most challenging areas of the diamond mentality, but it is not impossible. The diamond mentality gives you all the tools that would help you to quickly overcome the stress and possible depression from grief and put you back in control of your life.

First, you need to incorporate principle number one, acceptance, into your life. Death will happen to everyone, and there is nothing you or I can do about it. Therefore, accept the things you cannot change. In fact, the prayer by Theologian Reinhold Niebuhr is very good to live by and implement here; you don't need to be religious to embrace this prayer. It is good and helpful for everyone: "Lord grant me the serenity to accept the things I cannot change, the courage to change the things I can, and the wisdom to know the difference."

You cannot change death; it will happen to all of us, so it is important to accept that death is a part of life. Instead of asking, "Why me?", you should try asking yourself "What would my loved one want me to do now that they are gone?" I am sure if they could answer, they would say they want you to be happy. They want you to continue to live life to the fullest. They want you to be a help to others. When we accept that death is a very important part of life, we can prepare for it so that it does not catch us unawares.

We humans sometimes forget that we didn't create the world. We didn't make the rules. God did, and there is nothing we can do about it. Therefore, accept death the same way we accept gravity. If you throw a dangerous object above your head, it will come down and hurt you. You know that, and you acknowledge that. Therefore, you do not throw dangerous objects above your head. The same is with death. At some appointed time, each person will die, and there's nothing they, or you, or I, can do about it.

Once you have accepted death, then you are well on your way to recovery. You just need to embrace the other principles of the diamond mentality, especially emotional control and positive thinking. With the death of a loved one, our emotions tend to want to take control and lead us into depression. You have control over your emotions, so exercise dominion over them, so that you do not become depressed. Positive thinking helps to clear your mind and to put things into perspective. It also prevents you from having depressing and suicidal thoughts. If you can use the diamond mentality to overcome the pitfalls of the death of a loved one, then you can use the diamond mentality for anything that life may throw at you.

Sickness

Sickness is one of those things that no one wants. Unfortunately, none of us have any control over whether we become ill or not. We are powerless over sickness. It doesn't matter how educated we are or how much money we have or don't have, sickness affects people from all walks of life and every ethnic background. We try to convince ourselves that we are in control, but we are not.

Sickness sometimes hits suddenly and without warning. As a result, we are sometimes caught off-guard. Sickness causes a great deal of stress to those suffering from the illness and those close to them. It doesn't matter how "well" we eat or how much we exercise; we have no sure way to stop sickness from invading our bodies.

There are numerous sicknesses, some common and some rare, some curable and some incurable. We don't know what will afflict us. There are indeed some illnesses that you can prevent yourself from catching, but most of those are from the contagious category. Meaning you can catch them from another person. So, you can avoid a person with the contagious sickness, and most likely, you wouldn't get it. The main key here is that you need to have the knowledge that the person has the illness.

There are two areas of sicknesses that we stressed over the most regardless of the type of sickness. Those two areas are incurable illnesses that are life-threatening and illnesses that require surgery. The underlying reason is that we don't want to die. Hence, we are stressed when we have a life-threatening illness, or we need to have surgery. Some countries spend billions on medical research. According to a report from *Research America*, the United States spent $171.8 billion in 2016 on medical and health research and development.

I remember the story of Greg, who was from Illinois. Greg was a multimillionaire married to a wonderful and supportive wife, and they had three children. Life was going very well for Greg and his family. Suddenly his youngest daughter Lana became ill. They took her to the family doctor, who recommended that she was further tested. She received many tests, but no one could figure out what was wrong with her. Her condition slowly worsened.

Greg and his wife did their research as well. They were willing to try anything. His daughter Lana was only twelve, and the doctor said that if her condition continued to get worse, she would die. The medication prescribed was only relieving the symptoms. Someone recommended to Greg, a doctor in Florida that had helped many when others could not. Greg called and made an appointment and flew his family down to Florida. The doctor did several tests on Lana over a three-week period. When all the results were back, Greg and his wife were called into the doctor's office; he informed them that Lana had a rare disease for which there was no cure.

Greg then donated money to do research into finding a cure for his daughter. The doctor knew how to treat Lana so that her life would be less painful. To do that, Greg and his family needed to move to Florida. It was all very expensive, with Greg spending millions every year to keep his daughter alive. Greg also had to give up his job. After several years, Greg's resources were depleted, and still no cure for Lana. Greg had sold his three houses and their two vehicles. Greg and his family had nothing left. They had moved from riches to rags. They had to depend on the Salvation Army for food and shelter. That's where Greg found God.

Lana was very close to death, and her parents had no more money. They didn't even have enough money for food. One of the volunteers at the Salvation Army took Greg to speak with her pastor. From that time, the church also contributed to Greg and his family's wellbeing. The pastor would personally pick them up for church every Sunday. Quickly, Greg got to know God, and he repented for all the wrong he had done and accepted Jesus Christ. Two months after his encounter with Christ, Greg reached his breaking point. He fell to the ground weeping and, in total humility before God, asked Him to please heal his daughter. Greg said, "The riches aren't important, I don't need that back; just heal my daughter." His daughter was back to excellent health by the end of the week.

The doctor confirmed that Lana no longer had the sickness. The family and all involved were overjoyed, and all of them turned their hearts to Jesus. Greg also became a millionaire again after some years, but he was a totally different person. He eventually became a pastor, and that was his breakthrough testimony. Greg received a miracle for his daughter.

Greg was fortunate or blessed, or whatever you want to call it. His family was totally stressed and depressed from that ordeal. The steadfast love that his family had for each other helped them to stick together. However, many stories do not end like this one, and the families are torn apart and end up losing the loved one. Regardless of your situation, the diamond mentality can help you to deal with it.

Acceptance coupled with a positive attitude and clothed in emotional control is essential in these situations. Accept that there is no cure for the illness or that the person needs the surgery; otherwise, their condition will worsen and definitely lead to death. Acceptance goes a very long way, and it is vital to start there. By accepting, controlling your emotions, and having a positive attitude, your brain is freer to look for and develop solutions to the problem. You are in a better position to see all the possibilities, including approaching God and asking Him for help, even if you are not spiritual. Never fight over things or circumstances that you cannot change. If there is something you can do to change it, then stop complaining and do it. Complaining never got anything done.

Finances or the Lack of It

It is said that the love of money is the root of all evil. Money is necessary for this life, but it should never control us; neither should it be your god. Money is necessary for shelter, clothing, and food, among other things, especially if you live the city life. If you're not on the grid, then money is not all that necessary. However, regardless of the country you live in, the economic structure is designed in such a way that you need money.

In this world that we live in, money has become a necessary evil. Those who don't have it, long for it, and those who have it are fearful that someone will take it from them. Many believe that money is the solution to all their problems, but that is far from the truth. Money cannot buy love, happiness, or respect. Money cannot buy good health.

On several occasions, while listening to the news, I heard the announcement that a multi-millionaire suffering from a prolonged illness has finally succumbed to it. When you are rich and famous, your dirty linen gets aired in public. The many unhappy wealthy persons that make the news is astounding. It is clear from all these glaring truths that money is not the solution to all.

Despite these truths about money, many would do anything to get it. Many get involved in illegal activities, sometimes resulting in the loss of their jobs, incarceration, and even death just to get lots of money. Is it worth it? At some appointed time, we all die and leave the same money behind.

However, there are some honest people, who despite working hard, just cannot make enough to meet all their living expenses. Then they are those who find themselves in an unfortunate position that resulted in them losing their life savings. These and other groups of honest persons sometimes find themselves broke.

Without money, we may not be able to maintain a roof over our heads, have a nutritious meal to eat, sleep in a comfortable bed or pay the doctor for medical help. Not being able to afford these things can cause a person to be really stressed and depressed. Financial problems are usually a big headache for most people that have them.

So how can you overcome the challenges of being broke? I have known individuals to become so stressed over the lack of money that they became sick. A lady once said to me: "I cannot sleep and I have a splitting headache because I haven't paid my bills for three months and I don't know where I am going to get the money from."

Another lady told me she got laid off from her job, and she wasn't able to get another one. Six months had passed, and still no job. The bank had sent her letters that they were going to foreclose on the house because of her failure to pay the mortgage. Her blood pressure had significantly risen, and she was seeing the doctor because of the health issues brought on by her stressful situation which was due to being broke.

It was shocking to read in a newspaper in 2009, about a man who got laid off due to his company folding-up during the financial crisis of that time. The story told of the man killing his wife, children, and himself with a gun because he felt he couldn't start over again. That is the pressure that society puts on us; we allow it, and in return, we put some of it on others.

You can overcome the challenges of being broke should it happen to you. The biggest enemy of resolving or minimizing the impact of financial problems is pride. Pride prevents you from seeking help about money. You are accustomed being independent, and now, all of a sudden, you are forced into a situation where you have to ask for financial assistance. You have never in all your life asked anyone for money except mum and dad when you were a dependent child.

For money problems, the first thing you need to do is to get rid of your pride. Pride will do you more damage than good. I know a particular guy who blew millions of dollars because of pride. Before you can implement the steps of the diamond mentality, you need to get rid of your pride.

Next, look at your situation and make two lists. One with the things you have some control over, and another with the things you have no control over. The things that you have no control over, you must accept that you have no control over them. Waste no time worrying over them as that can cause you to become depressed. A depressed mind will prevent you from thinking clearly, and in your situation, you need to be thinking clearly.

The things that you have some control over, you need to focus your energy on those. You will need to have a change of attitude at this point, and yes, you have control over that. This is all part of the steps of the diamond mentality. You need to have a change of attitude towards receiving help. There is nothing wrong with getting help. It is pride that prevents people from seeking or asking for help. You can get help with food from organizations like the salvation army. You can visit a food bank and get groceries for your family. You don't need to go hungry. These organizations are there to help people in difficulty so that you and your family do not go to sleep hungry.

I remembered Yosef, who had told me his story. When you look at Yosef, you will never think for a moment that he had ever experienced financial difficulty. He carried himself well, was intelligent, and drove a nice car; dressed well; and was a committed family man with one child. The fact that we hardly knew each other and he told me about his past difficulties indicated he was a very humble person.

Yosef told me he got into financial problems after a few years of moving to Toronto from the Philippines. He had no money to buy food, and he and his wife would go to the food bank to get groceries. That helped them to put food on the table while the little money they made from odd jobs went to pay the rent for the basement apartment they lived in. It was a very stressful time for them, he said.

After some time, Yosef managed to get a better-paying job and was able to get back on his feet. He admitted to me that he partied hard when he first arrived in Toronto; going to parties multiple times per week. That had burned his money, and he had now come away from those activities. At the time Yosef was telling me his story; he had just completed building his home in the Niagara region and was going to leave Toronto in a few weeks to move there with his family.

In such situations, the diamond mentality will help to reduce your stress level considerably. Living on your own with a wife and child to support and having no money and no job is a super stressor. That is a situation that requires all six of those principles to manage it successfully. By applying these six principles to this type of problem, your mind is more at ease, helping you see all the possible solutions.

Now that you have changed your attitude and you are getting the help that is readily available. You can now put plans in place to get out of your situation. You can apply for jobs or upgrade your skills. You can even tap into your talents and look at opening your own business. There are always options available, but your mind must be at ease to see them. The diamond mentality helps to put your mind at ease. Take whatever job that is available as long as it is honest work. You never need to get into anything illegal or immoral. Once you are back on your feet, you can do like Yosef and move to a better-paying job.

With the diamond mentality, you can handle any criticism you may get. Some people are very insensitive. Never let them get to you. Instead, implement what you have learned in the chapter on criticism, and you will not be distracted or upset. You can control your emotions and think positively. Implementing all the steps of the diamond mentality will help you to overcome the challenges of being broke and getting back on your feet again.

The diamond mentality gives you the peace of mind that is essential to thinking quickly and effectively to develop a viable solution that will help you resolve your problems. When you are stressed, you cannot think clearly, and the resulting headaches contribute to clouding your vision, thereby making your situation worse. That is when you make more errors, become unproductive, unfriendly, and many more negatives. The diamond mentality gives you clarity of thought so that you are accurate, effective, efficient, and productive, and you can maintain your cool under any pressure.

Chapter 11
Conclusion

Ladies and gentlemen, life is worth living and living to the fullest. I don't know your passions or desires. Only you and God know what you are passionate about. What I do know is that you can become all that you desire to be. The road to your dreams may have many challenges and pitfalls that can deter you and distract you.

The diamond mentality will help you to overcome those challenges and pitfalls by equipping you with the tools to help you respond in a way that will eliminate or reduce the impact of stress in your life. Even if the road to your dreams is smooth and problem-free, you would still need the diamond mentality, as it helps you immensely when interacting with people and conducting business.

After you have achieved your dreams, you would still need the diamond mentality so that your life will be enjoyable, peaceful, and healthy. You can achieve your dreams and then later be plagued with a myriad of problems that can influence your health.

Don't settle for misery, unhealthiness, and failure. Choose today, choose now, to develop the diamond mentality and enjoy your partner, your children, your work, and your life. Simply enjoy life to the fullest!!

End

Bibliography

Allen, James. *As a Man Thinketh*. New York: *General Press*, 2018. PDF e-book.

Burg, Bob, Chapter 4. In *Adversaries into Allies: Win People Over Without Manipulation or Coercion*, 5. London: Penguin, 2013.

Dealing with Unfair Criticism? Responding Calmly and Rationally to Unwarranted Criticism. Management Training and Leadership Training—Online. Accessed November 12, 2018.
https://www.mindtools.com/pages/article/UnfairCriticism.htm.

Diamond Carat Size Chart. GIA Loose Diamonds. Accessed January 19, 2019.
https://www.lumeradiamonds.com/diamond-education/diamond-carat-weight.

Diamond Mining. The Environmental Literacy Council. Accessed January 19, 2019. https://enviroliteracy.org/land-use/mineral-resources/diamond-mining/.

Glover, Suzanne. *Benefits of a Positive Attitude: Today's Research.* Positive Thinking and Using Positive Thoughts—What Really Works? Accessed February 17, 2019. http://www.effective-positive-thinking.com/benefits-of-a-positive-attitude.html.

Hogg, Michael A., and Graham M. Vaughan. *Social Psychology.* Upper Saddle River: Ft Press, 2005.

Learn About Diamond Color. Anniversary Rings, Designer Engagement and Diamond Engagement Rings, Diamond Wedding Bands, Engagement Ring Settings. Accessed January 18, 2019. http://www.sunjewelry.com/diamond-education-color.html.

McLeod, S. A. (2014). *Attitudes and behavior.* Retrieved from www.simplypsychology.org/attitudes.html

Physical Effects of Worrying. WebMD. Last modified August 10, 2017. https://www.webmd.com/balance/guide/how-worrying-affects-your-body#1.

Plett, Heather. *Hold Your Tongue and Offer Your Heart Instead.* UPLIFT. Last modified July 5, 2017. https://upliftconnect.com/hold-your-tongue-and-offer-your-heart-instead/

Responding to Criticism. Working on Me | Be a Better Person. Last modified February 18, 2010.

http://www.working-on.me/personal-development/responding-to-criticism.

Serenity Prayer—God Grant Me the Serenity—Full Version. The Lords Prayer. Accessed March 15, 2019. http://www.lords-prayer-words.com/famous_prayers/god_grant_me_the_serenity.html#ixzz59U44UK5Q.

Stress & Anxiety Research. Tocris Bioscience | High Performance Life Science Reagents. Accessed January 16, 2019. https://www.tocris.com/research-area/stress-and-anxiety-research.
Stress and Heart Disease: Get Facts on the Warning Signs. MedicineNet. Accessed October 26, 2018. https://www.medicinenet.com/stress_and_heart_disease/article.htm#heart_disease_and_stress_introduction.

Wikipedia contributors. *Diamond Color.* In *Wikipedia, the Free Encyclopedia.* Wikipedia, The Free Encyclopedia., 2005. Accessed April 6, 2019. https://en.wikipedia.org/wiki/Diamond_color.

Wikipedia, the Free Encyclopedia. "Fight-or-flight Response." 2004. Accessed November 25, 2018. https://en.wikipedia.org/wiki/Fight-or-flight_response.

Wycklendt, Megan. *10 Simple Habits to Grow a Positive Attitude.* Fulfillment Daily. Last modified August 4, 2014. http://www.fulfillmentdaily.com/10-habits-to-grow-a-positive-attitude/

www.ingramcontent.com/pod-product-compliance
Lightning Source LLC
Chambersburg PA
CBHW070120260726
48658CB00001B/182